VALUES CLARIFICATION
FOR COUNSELORS

VALUES CLARIFICATION
FOR COUNSELORS

How Counselors, Social Workers, Psychologists, and Other Human Service Workers Can Use Available Techniques

By

GORDON M. HART, Ph.D.

Associate Professor
Department of Counseling Psychology
Temple University
Philadelphia, Pennsylvania

CHARLES C THOMAS • PUBLISHER
Springfield • Illinois • U.S.A.

Published and Distributed Throughout the World by

CHARLES C THOMAS ● PUBLISHER

Bannerstone House

301-327 East Lawrence Avenue, Springfield, Illinois, U.S.A.

© *1978, by* CHARLES C THOMAS ● PUBLISHER

ISBN 0-398-03847-3

Library of Congress Catalog Card Number: 78-15255

With THOMAS BOOKS *careful attention is given to all details of manufacturing and design. It is the Publisher's desire to present books that are satisfactory as to their physical qualities and artistic possibilities and appropriate for their particular use.* THOMAS BOOKS *will be true to those laws of quality that assure a good name and good will.*

Printed in the United States of America
V-R-1

Library of Congress Cataloging in Publication Data

Hart, Gordon M
  Values clarification for counselors.

  Includes index.
  1. Counseling. 2. Values. I. Title.
BF637.C6H353   361'.06   78-15255
ISBN 0-398-03847-3

To Judy,
whose care and sacrifice have often gone
unrecognized but have always been
needed and valued.

PREFACE

IN the fields of education, psychology, social work, and psychiatry there is an increasing emphasis on the preventative and developmental approaches to working with people. The training of human service workers primarily emphasizes remediation and rehabilitation of persons who are in the throes of a crisis or who suffer in a state of chronic emotional distress. Indeed, such persons need assistance from human service resources; however, a realization has developed that all people throughout the age span profit from learning experiences led by skilled practitioners. One preventative or developmental approach to interpersonal learning that has been used effectively with children, adolescents, and adults is values clarification.

Values clarification is the learning process by which people explore and clarify their values and establish plans of action based on their increased insight and knowledge about their values. Much of the literature on values clarification has consisted of lists of techniques that can be used by church group leaders, school teachers, playground supervisors, and other social service professionals. Unfortunately, there has been little description about how such professionals should implement the techniques that can be selected from these compendiums of exercises. It is important to keep in mind that any technique may relieve boredom or stimulate discussion when sprinkled into a class or group, but no technique used randomly can accomplish the purposes of the values clarification process or any preventative or developmental approach to interpersonal learning.

Values Clarification for Counselors is designed to help the social service professional, referred to by the generic term *counselor*, effectively implement values clarification techniques in

vii

an ongoing process of interpersonal learning. In Chapter I, "A Rationale for Working with Values," the nature and purpose of values in the lives of all of us is discussed, and the usefulness of examining our values is examined. In addition, an overview of the values clarification process in practice is given along with particular benefits of using this approach with children and adolescents. In Chapter II, "Preparing to Use the Three-Stage Values Clarification Process," the three stages of the values clarification process are described, and the usefulness of the process with individuals or groups is discussed. The steps in preparing to conduct a values clarification group are specified with particular emphasis on the first meeting of the group. Chapter III, "Using the Prizing Stage," Chapter IV, "Using the Choosing Stage," and Chapter V, "Using the Acting Stage," contain a description of the values clarification process. Guidelines are presented for selecting, sequencing, and conducting a discussion following values clarification techniques. This organization and emphasis on practical skills is based on the expressed needs of many human service professionals who have asked for assistance in their work with the values clarification process.

One student, Tony Collis, asked me when I was going to put my ideas into book form. From that point I began to work on this book, and Tony worked on his doctorate with a dissertation on values clarification under my direction. I appreciate his suggestion and his ongoing intellectual and emotional support. I would also like to recognize the many students whom I have supervised during their master's degree program who have shared their successes and failures in using values clarification techniques. Their honesty and creativity are reflected throughout this book. Most especially I acknowledge Judy, Keith, Brian, and Beth, who comprise the primary environment in which my values are challenged and supported, confronted, and strengthened. I appreciate and value them.

CONTENTS

VALUES CLARIFICATION
FOR COUNSELORS

A RATIONALE FOR
WORKING WITH VALUES

VALUES have been studied extensively, but seldom has there been a consistent effort to explain their relationship to behavior or to help individuals examine the relationship of their values to their behavior. In this chapter I will describe a point of view regarding the nature of values in human lives and how people can be assisted in examining their values and behaviors. In the first section I will describe the theoretical position that I believe underlies the values clarification process. In the second section I will examine the purpose of the "clarification" of values and its importance. In the third section I will present an overview of the values clarification process in practice and the benefits for children and adolescents.

The Nature of Values

In this discussion I will draw most heavily upon the work of Milton Rokeach, whose recent work (Rokeach, 1968 and 1973) appears to be the most comprehensive summation of the nature of human values. His work includes input from the fields of philosophy, sociology, and psychology. The foundation of his work rests on the belief that values are an extremely important independent variable in human behavior.

Rokeach has described a value as "an enduring belief that a specific mode of conduct or end-state of existence is personally or socially preferable to an opposite or converse mode of conduct or end-state of existence" (Rokeach, 1973, p. 5). A value system is "an enduring organization of beliefs concerning preferable modes of conduct or end-states of existence along a continuum of relative importance" (Rokeach, 1973, p. 5).

Values are a cognitive component of human beings, which

3

are learned as we grow from childhood to adulthood. We learn certain beliefs from our parents and other sources regarding honesty, love, and beauty. In this sense, values are a dependent variable and are affected by factors such as one's parents, peers, and culture. Not only does a person learn values but also that some values are apparently more important than others. A child raised in a strongly religious home may learn that salvation is more important than social recognition. Therefore, people develop a hierarchy of values that vary in terms of their relative importance. Although we certainly learn about values as adults, most of our learning takes place as children and adolescents.

In the definition of values there are two parts mentioned — a specific mode of conduct and an end-state of existence. Those values such as independence, responsibility, and self-control, which refer to modes of conduct, are called instrumental values. This means that a person has some values that have a direct bearing on how he lives each day. All of the decisions we make every day are affected by those instrumental values we hold. Through our upbringing, we have been taught that it is important for us to behave in ways that are, for example, helpful, intellectual, obedient, or possibly many others. We have also learned that we will be rewarded by our parents and others if we behave in ways that these significant others judge to be consistent with certain values.

Those values such as freedom, salvation, a world at peace, or equality are values that refer to an end-state of existence and are called terminal values. These terminal values represent long-range beliefs that we hope for, anticipate, or work toward. As is the case with the learning of instrumental values, we learn some vague and abstract notions of ideal or ultimate states of development that are supposedly valuable or satisfying to attain. Even though we may not be told what daily behaviors will achieve these end-states, the ideals are taught to us nonetheless.

For purposes of conceptual simplicity, it is assumed that our values pertaining to daily behavior are "instrumental" to achieving certain end-states of existence. The degree of correspondence between our instrumental and terminal values probably varies from person to person. A person who has some consistency between his instrumental and terminal values may act differently than a person who has little consistency between his instrumental and terminal values. The effects of instrumental values upon our daily activities are conceptualized as being different than the effects of terminal values.

Rokeach ties values to needs by stating that values are the "cognitive representation" of needs. Each daily situation in which we are faced with a choice of behaviors or a conflict to resolve provides us with a time to examine the situation in light of our values. In most instances a terminal value of national security will not have an effect on whether we send money to a charitable institution for orphans. However, if the decision concerns voting for one of several political candidates, a terminal value of national security might be important in terms of what the candidates believe about defense spending or foreign policy. Instrumental values are probably more important in a day-to-day way for most children and adolescents whose terminal values may not yet be clearly formulated and whose primary concerns are of a short-range nature.

The relationship between values and behavior cannot clearly be understood without mentioning attitudes. Whereas values refer to general modes of behavior or end-states of existence across situations, attitudes are tied to specific events, persons, or objects. Values are more central to a person's belief system and are not as easily changed as attitudes that can be changed by a new experience in life. There are probably far fewer values than attitudes. A schematic portrayal as in Figure 1 may be helpful in showing the relationship between values, attitudes, and behaviors.

Values are conceived as being more basic and resistant to change than attitudes. Attitudes are the beliefs that represent values in daily events with specific persons and objects. A person may place much importance on his value of equality of man, have attitudes about minority people such as their right to equal pay, housing, etc. and finally act in ways such as

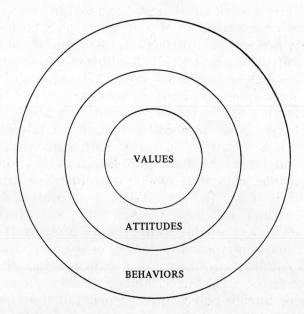

Figure 1. The relationship between values, attitudes, and behaviors.

supporting certain political candidates and hiring minority people in his business.

Figure 1 does not show the hierarchical fashion in which each person orders his values. This ordering is called a value system. The value system is formed by the learning of values from significant others plus a person's experience in daily activities offering data that confirm or disconfirm the appropriateness of the value ranking. As a child or adolescent engages in independent activities in his environment, he is exposed to values that may be in agreement or in conflict with those he has already learned. The effect of this interaction can be to strengthen the ranking of certain values or to change the ranking of other values.

The sources of data regarding values for children and adolescents are friends, teachers, television performers, sports heros, and literary characters both fictional and nonfictional. In our present society there are a variety of values expressed that are often in conflict with each other. Establishing a relatively stable system of values can be difficult for a young person amid a myriad of values from many sources.

The Purpose of "Clarification" of Values

The purpose of "clarification" of values is educational. Unlike theories of counseling and psychotherapy, which are designed to change personality, attitudes, and behavior, the values clarification process is designed to help children and adolescents to identify their values and examine the relative importance of their values, i.e. their value system. The assumption, which needs empirical validation, is that once young people have identified their values and the relationship of them to behaviors, they will be better able to cope with the conflicting sources of data regarding values that they receive from their friends, television, and other sources. It is further assumed that if young people learn about the acquisition of values they will behave in a more evaluative, logical, and consistent manner. This evaluative, logical, consistent manner does not deny spontaneity but implies that conflicts can be resolved quickly and decisions made with relative ease.

The educative efforts of teachers, counselors, and others using the values clarification process will be primarily focused on the building of skills to help young people cope with the conflicts or discrepancies between the values they hold and the values espoused and demonstrated by others. Of course, many young people have already experienced this conflict and need individual counseling to resolve their conflicts, which have resulted in emotional and/or behavioral problems needing concentrated efforts by skilled professionals. Overall, the values clarification process was designed to help young people who have not experienced severe problems.

A key point in this educative process is the belief that young people have the cognitive ability to examine their values, the relative importance of their values (value system), and the values of others. I believe that young people have this ability and can make such examinations in a simple and concrete fashion. As they grow older they will be able to deal with a greater quantity of data and data of a more complex and abstract nature.

Furthermore, if young people are able to clarify their values at one point in time, they may be able to use the skills of identification and analysis later in their lives. Some of Rokeach's research indicates that values do change in their importance as people grow older, change to a different socioeconomic class, and accumulate experiences. The clarification of values may be needed at several stages in a person's life if conflicts are to be resolved in a satisfying manner. The hope of all education is to provide immediate assistance to people and to provide skills for later life. This is certainly true of the educative process called values clarification.

Overview of Values Clarification

One way of clarifying values that has considerable merit is the values clarification process described by Raths, Harmin, and Simon (1966). They believe that there are three stages through which a person should pass in order to clarify his values. These stages are prizing one's beliefs and behaviors, choosing one's beliefs and behaviors, and acting on one's beliefs. Each state contains several substages, which are as follows:

Prizing   (a) Prizing and cherishing
            (b) Publicly affirming when appropriate

Choosing (a) Choosing from alternatives
            (b) Choosing after consideration of consequences
            (c) Choosing freely

Acting   (a) Acting
            (b) Acting with a pattern, consistency, and repetition

The derivation of these stages and substages is not explained by Raths and others of his colleagues, and so I will rely on my own interpretations of what they mean.

The three main stages seem to represent a process of identification, refinement, and application. The *prizing* stage seems to be a gross labeling of what a person values or thinks is important for him. People seem to operate on some sense of what is important to them, but there are areas in which they are unsure of what is important to them. Children and adolescents often need this stage, since they have had little opportunity to talk about and examine what is important to them. This stage makes their implicit values more explicit and, therefore, more available for examination, evaluation, and possible modification. I believe that this stage is very important, especially for children and some adolescents who have not done much introspection or examination of what is important to them.

The *choosing* stage appears to be one in which people make finer distinctions among their stated values and then order them in some priority fashion according to the strength or importance of each one. Where the *prizing* stage is concerned with identification in words or labeling, the *choosing* stage is concerned with comparisons and what makes some behaviors more attractive or rewarding or satisfying than others. This stage reflects a view that we should adopt values and their concomitant or resulting behaviors based on the rewards that these values or behaviors bring to us. Behaviorists say that we do this without much discussion anyway, and other behavioral scientists cannot disprove their theory. Raths would like us to make our choices more effectively, and his subprocesses help to do this. By choosing freely, from alternatives, and with knowledge of the consequences, I believe that people would be more satisfied with their values and behaviors.

Both in the *prizing* and *choosing* stages, Raths uses the words *beliefs* and *behaviors* without indicating their relationship or any differences between them. I believe that there is a definite relationship between these terms as I described earlier in this chapter. In my opinion, the entire values clarification process would be more understandable if the *prizing* and *choosing* stages focused on beliefs and left behaviors to the *acting* stage. The counselor would certainly discuss behaviors in the *prizing* and *choosing* stages but only as a means of getting to the notion of values; in essence a way of showing people how to identify and reorder their values by looking at a few sample behaviors.

The *acting* stage is designed to help people translate their values into observable behaviors. The term *values clarification* does not imply such action to me, but I believe in action rather than inaction in most cases, so I am in favor of the *acting* stage. This stage may be the most important for some persons whose values are and have been clear but who have not quite done anything about them or known how to do so.

With this brief overview in mind, I would like to describe the benefits of using each stage in working with children and adolescents.

Prizing

Stated in different words, *prizing* means, "What do I believe is valuable for me in an inherent or an instrumental sense?" An object has inherent value if it is in some way pleasing in and of itself. Paintings are examples of objects that have aesthetic value, a type of inherent value. On the other hand, some things have instrumental value for people, which means that the object helps bring about or achieve other objects. A car salesman's cars have instrumental value, since they will keep him in business. Some people paint because it is fun or relaxing (inherent), while others paint to get a picture to sell (instrumental). Some people play baseball for fun (inherent), and others play baseball to maintain their health, to avoid painting their house, or to get to know their neighbors better (instrumental). Raths seems to emphasize the instrumental nature of values throughout the values clarification process, which is fine for those who need such assistance. I would like to have the emphasis placed on a philosophy that encourages aesthetic values particularly without the necessity of asking, "What will these objects, values, or behaviors achieve for me?" Such an emphasis might help us to deal with the disenchanted youth and adults who have increasing amounts of leisure time but are restless and dissatisfied with all sorts of hobbies, entertainment, and recreational activities.

The *prizing* stage of the values clarification process is easily accomplished by some people. For example, children choose a cookie or ice cream with relative ease. They may also decide to play football or watch television with no apparent difficulty. The prizing of values becomes more complex when marriage, career, and associates are affected by one's values. I do not mean to imply that a person's career, marriage, etc. are decided at a particular point in life such as high school graduation or when a person proposes marriage. Our life-styles, including job, marital status, etc., are probably a result of an accumulation of experiences from early childhood plus some inherent factors and uncontrolled chance factors. Furthermore, I do not mean to imply that a child's decision over sharing a toy is any less stressful than an adolescent's choice of a high school curriculum or an adult's choice of a job. Indeed, we, as sage observers of life, might judge any of these decisions to be unworthy of distress, but we will not convince the person who is making the decision that he is not distressed. It is important to consider other people's decisions as important to them as your decisions are to you.

The *publicly affirming* substage of the *prizing* stage seems to be the time for a person to tell others what he values, which may be quite important for some people. Some young people are action-oriented, not thinking-oriented; that is, they act with little forethought, while others contemplate before doing anything. The action-oriented person may gain some rather startling insights about himself by stating what he believes and values in a passive group situation. This *public affirmation* substage may also help the person who has definite values but has not stated them aloud and thus not made them available for inspection by himself and others. The inspection might lead to changes in his values or to feeling more secure and confident about his values. This substage could also help the timid person who has not spoken about his values and could lead to his having more confidence in what he believes or values.

Benefits for Children

The techniques in *Values Clarification*, by Simon, Howe,

and Kirschenbaum, that are associated with the *prizing* stage show kids that they do have preferences for certain things and that they value some things more than others. I believe that once they see that they have preferences regarding concrete matters such as reading and playing they are better prepared to express themselves regarding more abstract concepts such as competition and friendship.

Another benefit is that they will see that others have values that are different from theirs. Too often children assume that everyone values the same things, which, of course, is not the case. This notion of individual differences can help to develop a sense of individual identity.

Benefits for Adolescents

The *prizing* stage will be of benefit to adolescents in ways similar to those described for children. The difference is that adolescents have more cognitive sophistication and can deal with abstractions better than children. Adolescents also will see that their values are based upon some feelings or preferences that are a part of them. In other words, their values are not assigned to them by outsiders but are an expression of their own being. It is not important to discuss how values are related to personality but just that our personalities and our experiences combine to produce our values.

In addition, adolescents move quickly from the objects or behaviors they prize to the abstract notions that represent a larger number of objects or behaviors. Moving from doing favors to friendship, getting an *A* in science class to achievement are examples of such shifts from low to high levels of abstraction. The specific objects such as a new basketball or specific behaviors such as dating are value indicators. They suggest or point to a more general concept called a value.

A preference for a single value indicator does not guarantee that a person holds the indicated value. Adolescents come to realize that values are a collection of value indicators and are a convenient way of expressing themselves. In other words, we can talk about honesty rather than list a dozen behaviors that most people would believe indicate honesty.

Some adolescents learn that they use a general concept or value term to describe themselves and are doing none or very few of the behaviors that indicate that value. Indeed, some persons have said they value cooperation over competition, yet upon doing some of the values clarification techniques they learn that they act competitively and like competition more than they act cooperatively and like cooperation. This may sound like a mere redefining of terms, but it is quite important to an adolescent who has been using a certain term to describe himself and now discovers that he does not actually act in ways to warrant that term. The reverse can also be true where an adolescent believes that he is bad (dishonest, antisocial, or whatever term has been used by his parents or peers) and yet he learns that he values honesty and acts in ways that most people believe are honest.

Another benefit is that adolescents will see values expressed in a variety of daily activities such as attending school, relating to friends, etc. They will see how their values are expressed with some degree of consistency from situation to situation. Overall, prizing gets adolescents off on a concrete note by labeling objects and behaviors they prefer and helps them begin to use more general terms that serve as representatives of such objects and behaviors.

The strategies used with children and adolescents to help them "prize" what they believe are powerful ones. The content of such a group meeting together with a counselor is the values and beliefs of the young people themselves with no textbooks, tests, or material to memorize. The *prizing* stage capitalizes on what I have seen among young people to be a need to express their feelings and beliefs, to compare with each other, and to grow in security and to relate closely to each other. Some will be hesitant to self-disclose, which is risky to be sure; however, the nature of the *publicly affirming* substage is to help young people take the risk that will bring about increased confidence and lead to increased clarity of values.

Choosing

The *choosing* stage is one where finer comparisons are made, an analysis of consequences is made, and sources of influence are examined. Some counselors focus on one of these three substages of the *choosing* stage but often do not proceed in a very comprehensive fashion. In the *choosing* stage the question is asked, "Given the options presently open to me, which course of action or specific behavior shall I choose?" This emphasis on behavior comes too soon for me. I would rather examine different values or beliefs concerning a specific situation, then look at the behaviors and their consequences in terms of feelings and tangible rewards or punishment. For example, the topic of parents might be introduced. I would suggest that each person in the group give his belief about appropriate child-parent relationships. Next, we would go into specific problems of establishing and maintaining good child-parent relationships and what actions we might take to achieve positive results and minimize negative results.

As in this example of parents, I feel comfortable by hypothesizing an ideal relationship or desirable situation and then figuring out what actions can achieve the ideal. I believe that this procedure is not different than the way we survey our individual clients for what they really want to be and then establish goals with them that may bring about their aspirations. Let us take a closer look at the three substages of the *choosing* stage and how they work.

Choosing from alternatives is the substage listed first and is important for several reasons. The techniques associated with this substage, such as "Alternatives Search" and "Brainstorming," show people that alternatives do exist. For some young people this simple notion is quite a revelation. Frequently, we react very emotionally and have trouble seeing alternatives, or else the pressure from other people to act in certain ways keeps us from seeing alternatives other than theirs. The skills of developing alternatives can be learned. Of course, some people are more creative than others and can generate alternatives with ease, while other people have great difficulty in doing so. A combination of both creative and noncreative young people in a group would be an ideal learning situation.

In general, this substage is an attempt to make young people examine situations and all the alternatives before they decide what to do. This takes some level of maturity, of course, but many children are able to think in terms of alternatives and so are helped by the techniques involved with alternatives.

Once alternatives are generated, these alternatives and their consequences are examined. In the *consequences* substage we examine the cost of each alternative. Each alternative course of action has some positive and negative consequences, and everyone would like to pick the alternative with the most positive and the least negative consequences. One difficulty is that a person may lack the experience and sophistication to anticipate the consequences of his actions. This substage is designed to help such a person. The acitivies in which he and the rest of his group participate will help him learn from the experiences of others. As we know, one of the powerful results of counselor-led groups is that participants learn from others without having to experience all aspects of life firsthand. For example, Tom might say that he would like to study more so he can get higher grades. Sue and Tim might point out that if he studies more then he will not have as much time for fun or recreation. Now Tom must decide whether his alternative of studying more is worth it.

Another goal, in addition to learning what consequences are possible, is to develop a better future-time perspective. The exercises used will help participants to anticipate reactions to their actions and to look beyond the immediate consequences to the long-term consequences. Some young people have a future-time perspective that is perhaps a week long. This may need to be lengthened if they wish to achieve the long-term positive consequences of their actions.

There is a further difficulty involving a person's perceptions of possible consequences. Some people may view a certain consequence as positive while others in the group view it as negative or at least not very positive. For example, Tom might say that he would like to get higher grades so his teacher would like and respect him. Others in the group would not care about their teachers' feelings about them. At the times when these points of contrast arise, a real impasse can occur in the group if the leader does not intervene. I suggest that the leader help group members to accept such opposing points of view as being equally valid and as examples of individual differences in values. By allowing others to have their values, a person has made a big step toward a firm set of values for himself.

Despite the difficulties involved in this part of the *choosing* stage, young people can begin to develop a sense of power over their own lives once they see that they can choose which action to take, that they have options, and that each option brings about certain positive and negative results. It is a powerful stage especially when coupled with the *choosing freely* substage, which is described below.

The last substage of the *choosing* stage is called *choosing freely* and deals with independence. Let us put aside, for a moment, the debate over free will and determinism of man. If Larry's parents tell him not to play with other children in the neighborhood and he complies, then his choice has been influenced by the opinions (wishes, orders) of his parents. The point of this substage is not to teach people about an existential position of independence but to help them become aware of influences on them and to evaluate the strength of these influences.

An example of gaining awareness of influences and evaluating them is the case of Judy. Judy's friends have urged her to smoke marijuana, but Judy states to her counselor that these sources of influence are nonexistent. If she honestly evaluates these sources via some appropriate values clarification technique or discussion within a values group, she may become aware of these influences and their impact on her behavior. Then she may be more likely to act on her values, not the values of others. Adolescents often choose, unfortunately I believe, to do those things that may be harmful but gain status or friendship with peers, which is of prime importance in the life of an adolescent.

Throughout the values clarification process, there is a premium placed on decisions made without coercion, as described above in the example of Judy, or self-delusion. The self-delusion is evident when you say you are going to join the ecology club because you believe in the concept when you are really joining to please your friends. Judy, in the example above, could have been unaware of the existence or power of her friends' influence, or she might have been aware but unwilling to admit the influence.

If she has trouble admitting influence, perhaps she could join a group with a different goal. Referrals by the counselor from values clarification groups to self-growth or problem-solving groups are quite appropriate and desirable.

For some groups of young people, this substage may open discussion of the ethics of various groups of people such as parents, peers, or teachers or the influence of situations on ethics. However, the most important result is a person who is aware of the influences upon him, evaluates them, and then makes his decision without deceiving himself.

Benefits for Children

This stage is a difficult one for young children (below age 10) especially since so many decisions are made for them or else their alternatives are narrowly restricted by their parents. The entire discussion of alternatives, consequences, and sources of influence must evolve around areas in which the children do have options. For example, they can choose their friends to some extent. They determine their behavior in school and particularly on playgrounds, parks, streets, and other places away from the presence of influential figures. The examples should come primarily from the children themselves, not the leader. Focusing on the areas in which they presently make choices will help them learn these decision-making skills of this stage more quickly.

Another difficulty, which is perhaps more evident in the *choosing* stage than in the other two stages, is that lack of vocabulary, low cognitive ability, or lack of self-insight may prevent children from learning to generate alternatives, look at consequences, or assess sources of influence. It is possible to help such children, but it takes more planning, use of audiovisual aids, a more simple vocabulary by the counselor, shorter periods of instruction, and all the other tips for good teaching that are so valuable for good counseling. Of course, as children get older they may acquire the verbal skills necessary for effective use of the *choosing* stage, and there will be fewer difficulties in values groups.

I believe that this stage is important for children despite the stated difficulties, since it helps the youngster who behaves in a random, unplanned manner who is perhaps naive or unsophisticated regarding his freedom to act. In many cases random behavior is defeating, and planful behavior can bring about many more positive results. Such planned or purposeful behavior can encourage a sense of power in one's environment. Not that children will gain these feelings fully nor should they really, but using existing strength and using skills of discrimination and evaluation in small areas such as a school club may well prepare them for the critical points in their adolescence.

A further gain is that children begin to explore nontraditional or atypical ways of behaving. If we as counselors feel a sense of responsibility to encourage creative, progressive, or self-satisfying ways of behaving, then I believe we have an obligation to at least examine a wide range of behaviors. An obvious example is that if a little girl does not want to wear frilly dresses or play nurse then she should be allowed and even encouraged to explore other ways of behaving. A less agreed-upon example would be that of a child who wants to squander money, not save it in the best Puritan tradition of our country. Perhaps we can risk our own positions and encourage a diversity of behaviors among those who are our clients.

Benefits for Adolescents

This stage is perhaps more applicable for adolescents than for children, due to the ability of adolescents to plan ahead and to carry out their actions with fewer restrictions. Perhaps, this stage is more critical for adolescents than for children due to the enormous pressures on adolescents to "behave like adults" when they are still filled with memories of childhood. Furthermore, they face extremely important questions regarding job, marriage, friends, recreational activities, and other value indicators that shape their life-styles.

For most adolescents I believe that the *choosing from alternatives* and *choosing with knowledge of consequences* substages are not as important as the *choosing freely* substage. Perhaps it is because adolescents are so sensitive to influence from others, especially peers, and are so involved in establishing their independence from their parents. In some cases they may evaluate the consequences of a variety of alternatives and consistently choose the alternative where they will receive the most attention and acceptance from their friends disregarding negative consequences such as possible parental punishment, loss of school privileges, or even physical harm. If this is what they value, then we must accept their decision when made freely, from alternatives, and with knowledge of consequences.

Acting

The *acting* stage of the values clarification process consists of two substages, *acting upon the choice made* and *acting with consistency*. The entire *acting* stage helps young people to bridge the gap from the intellectual discussion of the values group session to the real world outside. We can assume that people will act on their choices, but often people need support and direction for implementing their choices. Such support and direction can easily come from a counselor and members of a values clarification group. The group can provide a place where actions are planned and even tried out via role-playing or other simulation exercises. Furthermore, the group can critique a member's actions when he reports the actions he made outside the group.

The *acting on choices* substage seems to be the time when children and adolescents discuss appropriate times and places for their actions to occur. They probably have been talking about actions during the *choosing* stage since they would not be able to talk entirely in terms of abstractions such as honesty and self-satisfaction during earlier group sessions. I am sure that you would have mentioned behaviors or value indicators throughout the *prizing* and *choosing* stages in order to keep the discussion from becoming too abstract. For example, if you had been discussing honesty during the *choosing* stage, I am sure you would have mentioned telling the truth to parents or dropping facades with peers as examples rather than waiting until the *acting* stage. Therefore, this substage is probably quite obvious to the counselor and the children in the group due to their previous discussions, which included specific behaviors or actions. With adolescents who have been talking in terms of abstractions such as beauty or peace, this substage is the place where they and you translate values into specific behaviors. Often you will need to have group members analyze their present behaviors or life-styles via an exercise such as an auto-biography to discover the degree to which they are acting in accord with the values they have chosen as being most important to them.

The *acting with consistency* substage is reasonable as long as consistency does not become rigidity or inflexibility. A young person could certainly benefit if he changed from behaving randomly to behaving consistently. Random behavior is an indication that a person does not learn from his experiences and is unaware that he has some degree of control over his actions. Acting with consistency does not mean that a person always relates to people in the same way, such as the peace-maker when arguments or fights occur. Indeed, a person who behaves so consistently (or rigidly I would say) seems to ignore the differential cues that occur from situation to situation. By ignoring the cues, he denies reality and inhibits spontaneity of actions.

However, most people do not behave completely rigidly or at the ends of the continuum of personality. You will probably find yourself helping most young people to behave somewhat more consistently, which will increase the probability of obtaining favorable consequences, which may make them happier.

Benefits for Children

The *acting* stage is of benefit to children, since they can break down behaviors into specific acts that can be practiced in the group and then tried outside the group. An example is making friends or being more friendly to peers. These are admirable actions, but how does a child carry them out if he has not learned the appropriate social skills? I believe that groups, with the help of the counselor, can identify and practice the skills of making an appropriate verbal greeting to a peer, of asking him to help you or offering your help to him, or resolving a conflict between the two of you. I once supervised a counselor working with a client who did not know how to greet a new student as a potential friend. The counselor and client practiced the words and analyzed the feelings of the client until the client could try the greeting with the potential friend. This behavioral rehearsal started with the goal to be accomplished (making a friend), led to specific behavior (verbal greeting), and was attained by practice (role-playing) in a nonthreatening environment (with the counselor).

Not all of the specific actions a group discusses need to be practiced in the group. Where the children recognize the appropriate actions and are not fearful of attempting them outside the group, no behavioral rehearsal is necessary. Such a rehearsal is particularly necessary where children are fearful and need to have their anxiety reduced. By practicing behavior in a nonthreatening or minimally threatening environment, anxiety will be reduced to the point where they will attempt the actions outside the group.

Consistency is difficult to attain with children below age eight, and I would not be interested in trying to apply the *acting with consistency* substage with them. Frankly, I would only be interested in applying this substage with children who were markedly random in their behavior. Otherwise, I would wait until adolescence before looking for much consistency.

Benefits for Adolescents

The message from the originators of the values clarification approach is, if you believe in something, do something about it. And conversely, if you are not doing something, then you probably do not believe in it very strongly. I support these ideas, and I support active life-styles for people. However, I would certainly support a passive life-style for those who freely choose it.

The *acting* stage helps adolescents to translate abstract values into specific behaviors and then to list the steps one can take first, second, etc. to act consistently. This stage means that you as a counselor and the group will give emotional support to an adolescent who wants to behave in a certain way but is afraid of doing so. So often the fears that keep us from acting are exaggerated, but we never realize how exaggerated these fears are until we attempt the behaviors.

For both children and adolescents, the group can serve as a source of feedback when a person attempts some behaviors outside the group and then reports to the group on the outcome. Too often, groups terminate without being used for this feedback purpose, and the impact of the group is decreased. The group can provide suggestions for improvement if a member reports failure, and the group can further strengthen actions when a member reports success. We need to keep in mind that groups attain powerful reinforcement value for the members, and this power can be used profitably. In essence we are channeling powerful peer pressure or influence into the strengthening of behaviors that will be satisfying to each group member.

References

Raths, L., Harmin, M., & Simon, S.: *Values and Teaching: Working with Values in the Classroom.* Columbus, Merrill, 1966.

Rokeach, M.: *Beliefs, Attitudes, and Values.* San Francisco, Jossey-Bass, 1968.

Rokeach, M.: *The Nature of Human Values.* New York, The Free Press, 1973.

Simon, S., Howe, L., & Kirschenbaum, H.: *Values Clarification: A Handbook of Practical Strategies for Teachers and Students.* New York, Hart, 1972.

CHAPTER II

PREPARING TO USE THE THREE-STAGE VALUES CLARIFICATION PROCESS

MANY of the values clarification techniques are not original but come from Gestalt psychotherapists, sensitivity groups, and teacher training classes in colleges and universities. Those counselors who wish to use these techniques along with the techniques they are presently using may do so, but they are missing an important point. The point is that strategies help to achieve the goals of the values clarification process. By using techniques without considering the relationships between them and the three stages or factors of the process, a counselor is less likely to achieve the goals of the values clarification process. The three factors in the values clarification process can be used together to form a powerful aid to psychological maturity and independence.

The first factor that is found in the *prizing* stage is insight. Techniques are used that stimulate discussion centering on accurate identification and understanding of what a person believes is important or satisfying to him. The insight gained here will be used to help people make more realistic and potentially rewarding choices among the many conflicting values of our society.*

The second factor, which is in the *choosing* stage, is decision making. In this stage, skills are learned that can apply to any situation in life from choosing a mate to choosing a toothbrush. For some time counselors have complained that young people have problems deciding on high school courses, colleges, friends, and leisure time activities. I believe that the

---

*Incidentally, in *Values and Techniques* (Raths et al., 1966), the stages of the values clarification process are listed as choosing, prizing, and acting. In *Values Clarification* (Simon et al., 1972), the stages are listed as prizing, choosing, and acting.

choosing stage helps students to choose values that are appropriate for them and also teaches decision-making skills.

The third factor found in the values clarification process is behavioral counseling, which is contained in the *acting* stage. After a degree of insight has been obtained by means of the techniques used in the *prizing* stage and some decision-making skills have been learned in the *choosing* stage, a student is helped in the *acting* stage to carry out behaviors that he chooses. In the *acting* stage the counselor and the counselees translate values into behaviors that are consistent with the chosen values. The responsibility for what a person prizes, chooses, and acts on rests completely with the individual. This combination of insight, decision making, and behavioral counseling is a powerful process for young people.

Developmental Counseling Focus

In general, crisis counseling has not been overwhelmingly successful. Pressures of society, unfavorable family conditions, plus constraints upon counselors such as too many administrative and/or clerical duties and large client loads have kept counselors from being effective with the child or adolescent who needs remedial help. Indeed I view those clients who come to counselors in a dilemma or crisis as needing immediate symptom reduction or elimination and then perhaps long-range help. The person caught stealing lunch money from others can use help in getting through an immediate crisis plus help to avoid future crises.

The developmental counseling described by Blocher (1966) and others is designed to assist students in understanding themselves; in becoming mature, independent, and competent; and in developing satisfying relationships with others to name just a few goals of developmental counseling. The assumption is that everyone can be helped in their psychological growth by knowing their needs and ways of satisfying those needs. The contrast between crisis counseling and developmental counseling is obvious. I believe that the number of crisis cases will decrease if adequate developmental counseling is done.

Throughout this book I will be referring to the use of the values clarification process in a developmental counseling program. This is one where counselors select children or young people who have not identified problems or crises. These children are not the identified misbehavers or withdrawn children but are the vast majority of children and young people who can be helped to improve themselves with the help of counselors. Specific values clarification exercises can be taken out of the overall values clarification process and used with success in crisis counseling, but I will direct my attention only to the use of the techniques as they would be used in the developmental counseling framework.

Use in Individual Counseling

Some values clarification techniques can be used effectively in individual counseling. The techniques are good stimuli for discussion between the counselor and counselee and can be used as homework for the client to do between counseling sessions. Making an autobiography or keeping a diary are examples of techniques that have been used with individuals. "Incomplete Sentence Blank," "Value Survey," or "Miracle Workers" are other examples. Sometimes you may wish to have a client do one of these techniques in your office and discuss it. At other times you may wish to have the student do the exercise at home between counseling sessions. This use of techniques as homework helps the client to relate the in session discussion to his world outside the counselor's office.

Use in Group Counseling

The advantages of using the values clarification process with groups of children or adolescents are the same advantages as group counseling per se. Briefly, people in the group see that others are like them in some ways and that their ideas, feelings, or desires are not as unusual as they had feared. People also realize that each person is different from all others in the group. When group members accept these differences in persons, they will then be able to use each other to gain new points of view. There are certainly more available points of view in groups than in individual counseling.

Another advantage is that people have more sources of support and reinforcement available to them than in individual counseling. As mentioned in Chapter I, peer pressure is powerful and can be used by a skillful group leader to support those persons who need it. We often see that young people are more affected by their peers than by adults, and I suggest that counselors make use of this effect young people have on each other for positive outcomes. Of course, those outcomes would be ones that individual group members choose.

A further advantage is that a group can function as a practice field for trying out new ideas and behaviors on the rest of the members. In essence, the group can react as they would outside the counseling office but within the control and structure shaped by the group leader.

Even if you accept the general advantages mentioned above, remember that these advantages may not apply equally to all types of group situations. For purposes of semantic clarity, let me explain my use of the terms *group counseling, counseling group, values group, task group,* and *process group.*

Throughout this book, I will use the term *group counseling* to mean the counseling done by a counselor with a group of young people, with a focus on their concerns and where there is meaningful interaction among group members. I do not believe that the teaching or data transmission done by counselors concerning part-time jobs or upcoming achievement tests is group counseling. These groups are important, but I would call them guidance groups instead of counseling groups. In these guidance groups members usually talk about the data given by the counselor in a cognitive fashion with little interaction among the members. A counselor could certainly organize a counseling group to discuss concerns people have about jobs or tests, but the focus would change from the data itself to the attitudes and feelings of the group members about the data. I would call this latter group a *counseling group.*

Values group is a term I use when referring to those counseling groups that are developmental, not crisis, in orientation and that use the values clarification approach in a fairly systematic fashion. Throughout the three values clarification stages of *prizing, choosing,* and *acting* there is a task orientation rather than a process orientation. The task is not to solve a problem as in crisis counseling but to help young people delineate values, examine the choices open to them, and act in accord with their values. There is no emphasis on examining the dynamics of group variables such as trust or cohesiveness or factors such as communication styles, which I refer to as a process orientation. I believe that trust and cohesiveness should be encouraged but without making them central topics of discussion and analysis.

The advantage of a task orientation seems to be that the group members have a clear sense of direction or purpose from the very beginning. It also is easier for me as leader and for the members to evaluate the amount of progress they are making. The clearer the objective of the group, the easier to determine success or failure.

Use with Children and Adolescents

I have limited this book to those counselors who work with children and adolescents for several reasons. First, I am most familiar with children and adolescents, plus I work with counselors who work with children and adolescents. Second, I believe that these groups of young people are a vital part of our society and that if we can help them when they are young, we will have helped them for life. Prevention of problems later in life cannot be guaranteed, but I believe that it is worth our every effort. Finally, the values clarification approach was originally developed with these populations in mind. Adults may be able to benefit from the values clarification process, but much experimentation and revision need to be made before I could advise extensive use of the process with adults.

For most children, a values group will help them identify the people and activities that are important to them. It will help them realize that they do have some control over their lives as they make certain daily choices. It also will help them to try activities that they had not thought about or were hesitant to try. Since most children have some difficulty seeing the relationship between values and actions, their understanding during a values group will be incomplete. The group will be a starting point, not a culminating activity. Furthermore, they are under considerable control by their parents, who limit the choices the children would like to make. Parental control can be positive or negative, but the effect of the *choosing* stage of the values clarification process with children is severely limited by parental control.

The *choosing* stage is more effective with adolescents than with children due to the increased cognitive ability of adolescents and their increased freedom to make their own choices. One frequent drawback in working with adolescents is that they are aware of the many conflicting values in society and the innumerable choices open to them. There have been pressures on them as children from parents, the media, peers, and teachers, but now as adolescents they are more conscious of these pressures and their impact upon their values. Furthermore, adolescents enjoy their increased freedom, but also fear the responsibility of exercising such freedom when such a dazzling array of choices is open to them. The decision-making skills of the values clarification process are especially important for adolescents.

In conclusion, I believe that for both children and adolescents there is value in examining the relationship between what they believe is valuable and their daily activities. In other words, they can see that their beliefs direct their lives. By ordering their values and acting in accord with them, satisfaction can be attained. A related benefit for both children and adolescents is that they begin to see themselves as persons in progress, with a past that affects them presently and a future that they can determine. This sense of time enables people to exercise control over their lives rather than relinquish control to others.

I have used the term *counselor* to mean a person who functions as a professional or paraprofessional worker with children, adolescents, or adults. These workers are found in schools and community agencies and are labeled social workers, classroom aides, mental health workers, and others. Regardless of job title, many persons perform counseling functions with children and adolescents. It is these persons who can use the values clarification techniques in their work.

In addition to the direct counseling function with individuals and groups, counselors may perform other functions in the area of values clarification. One function is that of resource person to other members of your staff. Once you have learned the techniques of the values clarification process, you can communicate them to others. This communication may take the form of describing the process to others informally or demonstrating the techniques during a staff meeting. Other ways of serving as a resource person would be to collect lists of books, articles, and workshops on the use of values clarification techniques and distribute them to your colleagues.

Your colleagues might be school teachers if you are a counselor in a school. Or they might be houseparents, tutors, leaders at the YMCA's or YWCA's or other youth groups, church leaders who work with young people, probation officers, and others who interact with kids and adolescents on a regular basis. Let us look at schools for a moment. Teachers have been urged for some time to take part in the psychological education of their students (see *Personnel and Guidance Journal*, May, 1973). The values clarification process was originally developed for use in the classroom but with no notion that the school counselor could or should be the resource person for teachers wanting to use the techniques. I would like to see the counselor introduce the process and show the appropriate materials as found in Simon et al. (1972) and in Raths et al. (1966) to teachers.

Some counselors have demonstrated several techniques in a classroom while teachers observed. Later the teachers could use a technique with students while the counselor observed and gave helpful suggestions after the class.

In community agencies, a counselor can be a resource person in a way much like that of a school counselor. He can describe the process, circulate written descriptions of techniques, and perhaps demonstrate the techniques using his fellow workers to play the role of group members. Co-leading a group with one experienced counselor and one novice counselor is an effective way of learning to use the values clarification process. Some counselors have become participant-observers of their fellow workers as they begin a values group and then let their colleague on his own after the first several group meetings.

A final function of school counselors, in addition to direct counseling of students and giving resources to others, is the consulting with the planners of the school curriculum. Now that the post-Sputnik craze for science and mathematics is over, there is a strong movement toward relevance and the humanization of education via affective curriculum. This means that educators are trying to encourage responsible citizenship, economic independence, skills of leisure-time use, etc., not by memorizing names of political candidates but by examining the morality of political issues and helping students take a stand. This movement toward psychological education has been indicated by changes in curriculum such as a return to the homeroom, club period, and guidance period found in the secondary schools of the 1950s.

Another indication is the use of class discussions or class meetings led by the teachers on whatever is important to the students regardless of course content. This technique, made famous by Doctor William Glasser (1965, 1968) has been quite effective in promoting the psychological growth of adolescents. Furthermore, there are ways in which each subject matter course from algebra to chemistry can be modified to increase the focus on students' values (see Harmin, 1973). I believe that a counselor who is knowledgeable about the values clarification process can help to shape the goals of the courses plus provide techniques that may bring about these goals.

Before You Begin a Values Group

There are several suggestions that might be helpful for you to consider prior to your first values group. Many of these suggestions would pertain to all counseling groups and have been suggested by other writers in the group counseling field, but let me describe a few for you. As mentioned in Chapter I, you will not be effective if you try to impose your values upon the group members. This does not mean you should have no values, but know what they are and be able to accept values of others that are in contrast to your own. Once we are less threatened by people with different values, helping them clarify their values becomes easier. I suggest that you reveal specific values only if you are asked by the group for your position. The focus is on their values, not yours. I believe that indications of your values will become known to the group as they observe your clothes, speech, and actions. Denial of your values to the group is ineffective.

No matter what topic you are discussing, be specific, use examples, and have the group do so too. You must make all topics relevant to their world even if you do not always see the relevance to your world.

At times you will not understand their jargon, but do not stop a discussion to obtain definitions. Use your own words and try not to adopt their jargon as your own. Using their terms will always appear stilted and will affect your credibility with the group. A related point is to allow them to say what they want to say without censoring their language. If they are censored then they are not comfortable with you or the group. Some censoring will always go on, but hopefully it will be minimal.

The First Session

During the first meeting you will want to explain the purposes of the group; general guidelines such as meeting time, day, place, and confidentiality. I would explain to the group that I expect them to attend all sessions and be active participants. I do not tell group members that they may drop out at any time, but I allow them to do so. I have found that making an announcement regarding dropping-out leads to dropping-out.

Similarly, I believe that no one must participate in an exercise or activity. I do not tell people this, but if someone says that he or she would rather not do something, I immediately make him or her an observer? The observer watches others participate and then reports to the group on what he saw and how he felt. I make the observer an important role and use the data he gives. The observer would feel quite alienated and distant if he chose not to participate and did not report on what the others did. Sometimes in groups of children the observer role becomes a desirable one, and they ask to be an observer rather than participate. Quietly but firmly tell them that you want them to participate.

The number of sessions could vary, but I suggest a minimum of four weekly meetings with an optimum number of six sessions. The meeting time of each session should be a minimum of fifty to sixty minutes for children and up to ninety minutes for adolescents. Many of these guidelines can be explained to the young people individually before the first meeting of the group and then repeated during the first meeting. I believe that an individual meeting of the counselor with each potential group member is of value but by no means necessary as a screening device or as a motivator for members.

After the ground rules have been explained and discussed, you should list the stages and substages of the values clarification process and then explain the process. With many groups I list the stages and substages on a chalkboard and leave the board in view during all group meetings. The purpose of this visual aid is to make sure that the group members see their position in the process and can note their progress. This check on progress is much more concrete than entirely verbal descriptions of process as done in other counseling groups. Counselors and group members using the values clarification approach know where they are leading the group and what they have done to accomplish their goals.

 Even though the process is logical, there is a tendency on the part of some counselors to use many techniques, perhaps with the hope that the techniques themselves guarantee clarity of values. I believe that the techniques are fine but are primarily a stimulus for the group and that the real work is done during the discussion following a technique or exercise. It is during this follow-up discussion that the people can look at their value indicators, choices, and actions and help others examine theirs. I suggest that counselors have discussion questions ready using some of the questions found in Chapters III, IV, and V.

A discussion following a values clarification technique, as suggested above, may sound like a classroom procedure, but school counselors do not relate discussion to subject matter. Frequently, teachers of chemistry, biology, or general science for younger children bring in social issues concerning values such as ecology and use values clarification techniques accordingly. Counselors do not have such an obligation to subject matter and so must try to relate the exercises to the lives of each group member without the comfortable support of a social issue or course content. This lack of structure is a problem for beginning counselors and is perhaps the reason why they use so many exercises with so little discussion. Experienced counselors are happy to have a loose structure and one that can be modified through the selection of certain exercises or the addition/ deletion of exercises during the group sessions. If a counselor understands the values clarification process and has some experience in group counseling, he can use the values clarification exercises most effectively.

References

Blocker, D.: *Developmental Counseling*. New York, Ronald, 1966.

Glasser, W.: *Reality Therapy: A New Approach to Psychiatry*. New York, Har-Row, 1965.

Glasser, W.: *Schools Without Failure*. New York, Har-Row, 1969.

Harmin, M., Kirschenbaum, H., & Simon, S.: *Clarifying Values Through Subject Matter: Applications for the Classroom*. Minneapolis, Winston Pr, 1973.

———— *Personnel and Guidance Journal*, 51:581-691, 1973.

Raths, L., Harmin, M., & Simon, S.: *Values and Teaching: Working with Values in the Classroom*. Columbus, Merrill, 1966.

Simon, S., Howe, L., & Kirschenbaum, H.: *Values Clarification: A Handbook of Practical Strategies for Teachers and Students*. New York, Hart, 1972.

CHAPTER III

USING THE PRIZING STAGE

THIS chapter describes the use of the *prizing* stage of the values clarification process. Guidelines, discussion questions, and selected techniques are described for use with children and adolescents. Almost all of the exercises mentioned here are from *Values Clarification* (Simon et al, 1972), where the exercises are described but little is said about introducing, applying, and discussing them. I have modified most of the techniques mentioned in this chapter by rewording them so that they are clearer and by expanding the number of stems, situations, or alternatives to give counselors a wider range of options. As I mentioned in Chapter I, the exercises will be of little worth unless counselors are certain of how to use them.

The most important guideline for using the *prizing* stage with children is to be specific, and one way of being specific is to use concrete materials such as pencil and paper. Even if the exercise can be done verbally by the children, put questions and/or answers on paper for them and have them write or circle answers to questions. If you can make a verbal exercise into a pencil and paper one, do so. In addition, use pictures to set the mood or illustrate scenes. Most counselors who work with children keep folders of pictures taken from magazines.

Another way of helping to get the group moving is to make name tags for them using strategy number 19, "Ing Name Tags," which helps everyone remember names of other group members. You may find that during the discussion following the exercise, children will doodle with pencil and paper. I suggest that you collect the pencils when the exercise is completed to avoid distractions. If the papers become a distraction, have the children put their paper behind them so it will be out of the way but available for reference during the discussion.

Furthermore, keep the exercises and discussion moving at a pace that will keep everyone's attention. You will probably find yourself moving at a faster pace than you would with adolescents, who might discuss issues more extensively. At times it might seem as if you are teaching the children rather than counseling them. You may wish to put more responsibility on the group by encouraging more member-to-member interaction than member-to-leader interaction. The pace will be slower with the increased member-to-member interaction and the chances for getting off the subject will increase, but members will be more highly involved.

When you begin the group, you will discuss the guidelines such as meeting time, place, purpose, and then describe the stages of the values clarification process. All of this introduction conveys important material to group members but puts the counselor in a strong leadership position. When the counselor then begins the group by leading them in an exercise in the *prizing* category, the group again gets an impression of the counselor as teacher. This teacher-image often results in behaviors by group members such as raising a hand for permission to speak or speaking to the counselor rather than speaking directly to another group member. I believe that only one person in the group should speak at once, but I am also interested in member-to-member interaction. This interaction provides for the greatest amount of peer learning, practicing of social skills, and emotional support.

I work to become less of a teaching or authoritarian group leader and become more of a facilitative or democratic group leader by allowing brief discussions that are off the topic. Furthermore, I encourage members to take responsibility for discussion by asking them direct questions or by telling them to speak directly to other group members or by being silent, which usually allows others to speak. In addition, I often participate in exercises, which helps group members to see me as more of a co-participant.

I do not believe that members ever view an adult group leader as a full-fledged group member no matter what the leader does. The very facts that the group leader is an adult, is responsible for forming the group, and selects appropriate exercises are enough to keep the leader as a leader, not as an equal member of the group. He can be nondirective and have a loose structure in the group, which may be categorized as a laissez-faire role rather than an authoritarian role, but he never loses some degree of authority in the minds of the group members.

The values clarification techniques that I believe are most applicable to the *prizing* stage are listed here by the name and number assigned to them in *Values Clarification*. Several of the techniques are appropriate for more than one of the three stages and so are listed in Chapters IV and V as well as here. These techniques are also listed in the Appendix by number, name, and page number as they appear in *Values Clarification*, where they are described in detail.

The techniques most appropriate for the *prizing* stage are "Twenty Things You Love to Do" (1), "Values Voting" (3), "Rank Order" (4), "Either-or Forced Choice" (5), "Forced Choice Ladder" (6), "Value Survey" (7), "Values Continuum" (8), "Spread of Opinion" (9), "Values Whips" (10), "Proud Whip" (11), "Public Interview" (12), "Interview Whip" and "Interview Chain" (13), "Group Interview" (14), "I Learned Statements" (15), "I Wonder Statements" (16), "Values Journal" or "Values Data Bank" (17), "_____ Ing Name Tags" (19), "Magic Box" (34), "All About Me" (35), "Pages for an Autobiography" (36), "Unfinished Sentences" (37), "Who Comes to Your House" (38), "Strength of Values" (39), "Strongly Agree/Strongly Disagree" (40), "Taking a Stand" (41), "Personal Coat of Arms" (47), "Fallout Shelter" (48), "Cave-in" (49), "Alligator River" (50), "Rogerian Listening" (51), "Life Line" (53), "Who Are You" (54), "Epitaph" (55), "Obituary" (56), "Two Ideal Days" (57), "How Would Your Life Be Different" (60), "What Is Important — A Song" (61), "I Am Proud — Song" (62), "What's In Your Wallet" (63), "What We Know And What We Want to Know" (65), "Are You Someone Who" (72), "Reaction Statements" (76), "Diaries" (77), and "The Suitcase Strategy" (78).

For Use with Children

I introduce an exercise by telling the group that we are going to play a game that will help us know more about the things

we really like in our world. I use the term *game* with children
rather than *exercise, technique,* or *strategy,* which can be used
with adolescents. I also omit the term *values* and talk about
things we really like in our world and then give examples such
as playing ball or viewing pretty pictures. I then tell them the
name of the game or make up a name that they can remember.
You will find that they remember the exercises that are meaningful to them, and a vivid title helps their memory. With one
group the first exercise we did was "Either-or Forced Choice,"
where they had to pick one of the two opposite items and move
to the end of the room that represented the items. Pairs of items
such as Cadillac®-Volkswagen® and peanut butter-caviar were
used. For some reason the group always referred to that exercise
as peanut butter-caviar in later sessions. The name was as good
as "Either-or Forced Choice" and helped them remember what
they did in the *prizing* stage of the values clarification process.

Next I give the instructions on how to play the game and
quickly move into it with little time for questions. I allow little
time for questions so that the timid children do not have time
to devise complex questions as a stalling tactic. I get them
involved before their anxiety can bind them up. Questions will
quite likely arise during the more complex games, but they can
be answered without stopping the progress of the entire group.

Sometimes I admonish the group during a game to be sure to
say what is really important to them. This admonition would
come if I think that the children are saying or writing or selecting the socially acceptable value indicators or the value
indicators chosen by the rest of the group. This often happens
at the beginning of a values group when members are somewhat insecure and have a desire to be accepted by the rest of the
group. You will see this reliance of the group on each other by
their looking at each other's papers or by their waiting for
someone to respond and then agreeing. I suggest that you
spend more time getting to know each other better in order to
build trust among the members. Have the members introduce
themselves and describe themselves. Have them ask questions of
each other regarding their likes and dislikes. Set an example by
disclosing some of your personal life or feelings to the group.

Have them pair off to remind each other of the next session or to walk home together or to play together after the sessions. Once a degree of trust is established, which may take one or two sessions, go back to your values clarification emphasis.

Some values clarification techniques are less threatening than others. I believe that those with low threat should be used initially so that children can get to know you and the other group members with as little anxiety as possible. One example of an exercise of little threat is "What's In Your Wallet." In this exercise, people take something out of their wallet or bring something into the session of value to them and show it to the group. You may ask them to tell why it is of value. Two similar exercises are "Proud Whip" and "Values Whip," where each person tells of something he values or of something he is proud by saying, "I value . . .", "I'm proud of . . .". Some sample "Proud Whip" questions are as follows:

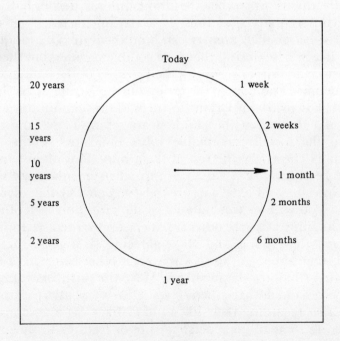

Figure 2. Time machine — future.

1. I am proud when I . . .
2. I am proud to be . . .
3. I am proud when I know . . .
4. I am proud when I go (go with) . . .
5. I am proud when I try (try to) . . .
6. I am proud when people say . . .
7. I am proud when I help someone by (to) (who) . . .
8. I am proud when I participate in . . .

An exercise similar to "Proud Whip" and "Values Whip" that is often used with individual children is "Time Machine." To make a time machine as shown in Figure 2, cut a piece of construction paper into a circle about 5 inches in diameter. Fasten the circle to an 8 1/2 by 11 inch piece of construction paper at the center of the circle with a fastener so the circle can turn. Around the circle on the construction paper, write in amounts of time such as one day, one week, two weeks, one month, six months, one year, two years, five years, ten years, fifteen years, and twenty years. Draw an arrow on the circle from the mid-

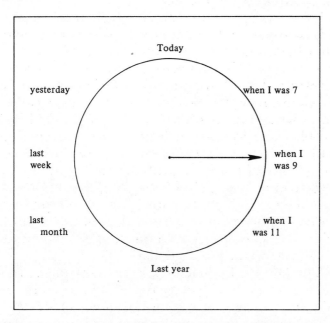

Figure 3. Time machine — past.

point to the edge like the minute hand of a clock. The circle is the selector of the time machine and can be operated by the child. Have the child set the time machine, then ask him what he is doing at that time in the future. Some counselors use two circles on their time machine, one for the future and one for the past as in Figure 3.

This exercise, when used at the beginning of a values group, elicits data from the children regarding their value indicators at various points in time. The future time machine will allow them to project themselves into roles as older children and share with the group what things (house, car, baseball, career, friends, independence) are important to them. Usually the things they are doing in the future are of some importance to them now. In a similar way the past time machine may be a nonthreatening way for children to describe the important events in their lives that have happened in the past. Most counselors ask the children what they liked to do at a specific time in the past or what they would like to do in the future in the case of the future time machine.

Another exercise of low threat is "Magic Box," where a box or bag is passed around the group and each member tells what he would like to have if this magic box could produce it for him. You can then ask each person to tell why his chosen item is important to him. A variation of "Magic Box" is to put the bag or box in the center of the circle of group members and have them write their item on a piece of paper. This helps to keep people from changing their item to one that someone else previously announced. Other exercises of low threat are "Either-or Forced Choice" (described earlier), "Values Continuum" (described later in this chapter), "Rank Order," and "Values Voting." In "Values Voting," the members vote yes or no by show of hands on a variety of questions asked by the counselor. An example of such a question is, "Would you like to have an important job some day?"

In "Rank Order" children are asked to rank three alternative value indicators such as having fun in a large group, having fun with a few friends, or having fun alone. This exercise can be done orally, but the counselor may need to write the three

alternatives on a chalk board so that children can easily remember the three options. Each child then tells his ranking of
the three choices. With children of adequate reading ability you
could put the three options on paper and have each child
number the options according to their importance. Most counselors use several (three to five) sets of rank orders and then
proceed to discuss the set that appeared to be the most stimulating to the group.

Some of the exercises of low threat that I have just mentioned
are simple, and others are a bit more complex. I usually start
with several simple exercises of low threat followed by several
more complex exercises. By planning the sequence of the exercises before the session, you can concentrate on the discussion
following the exercises.

Discussion Guidelines

After clarifying what is important to group members, you
may wish to have them describe the reasons why certain value
indicators such as baseball or reading are important. I might
contrast the things they like esthetically, such as things that are
appealing, pretty, fun, exciting, or tasty, with things they like
instrumentally, such as reading, which helps them in school. I
would also point out to the group that everyone in the group
valued or prized different things, and this was quite common
and acceptable.

Next, I would move into the area of public affirmation or
disclosure of their value indicators. In other words, do others
know about the things you value? If not, why not? If there is
some reason why you have not told your friends, parents, or
teachers about the things you value, what is the reason? And
finally, would you like to eliminate the reason and be more
open to others about what you prize? Some children reveal
more about themselves than others. I can accept those children
who do not reveal much about themselves, but I believe that
they would be better understood and better known by others if
they disclosed or affirmed their values publicly. Moreover, I
believe that when they bring the things they prize into the

open, at least with friends, they are likely to get a clearer picture of their value indicators.

Additional Guidelines

There are some additional guidelines that I follow during the exercises and during the discussion following the exercises. I assume that all children have some value indicators; that is, all of them have likes and dislikes. Some like books, football, and being with peers, while others like puzzles, ropes, and being alone. I encourage them to identify the activities and people in their lives that are important to them both esthetically and instrumentally. I reward them for these identifications by verbal praise. For some children I, as a source of reward, become an important person in their lives. The source of this importance is probably due both to my rewarding them for talking about themselves and my acceptance of their value indicators, which are different from my own.

Furthermore, I accept the names of people who are important to the children, but I always help them identify what it is that they like about the person or persons. Sometimes the children value people because they are famous or dress well or are good at sports in the usual way that children have hero figures. Sometimes children value certain people because they do things for them, such as buy them gifts or give them love or attention. I help them explore their reasons for valuing certain people because more global values such as fame, wealth, athletic competence, materialism, attention, or love can then be examined.

Finally, I have found that children can remember what happens in a values group if they keep a values notebook or folder where they collect the notes and papers completed during each session. At the end of each session each member puts any materials he used in a folder. Before the next session the counselor may have each member look through his folder to refresh his memory of what went on during the last session.

Usually the folders or notebooks should be kept in the counselor's office to avoid loss and insure privacy. However, most counselors reserve the right to examine the folders or note-books, since the material they contain has already been openly discussed in the group. I suggest that a counselor tell the group that this may be done between sessions as a memory refresher for the counselor. It is always better to tell the group before you do something rather than admit something after you have done it, such as examine their folders.

Older children who have adequate writing skills may keep a "Values Journal" in which they record their feelings and thoughts about the activities of each session. The journals may be kept in the counselor's office but should not be examined by the counselor. Some counselors do examine the journals between group meetings and tell the members that this is a way for them to communicate with the counselor. I believe that the purpose of values journals is to allow members an opportunity for free and unrestricted reactions. If members know that the counselor will read their journals, they will be less free with their reactions.

Some counselors allow time for discussing the journals at the middle or end of the series of values group meetings. This is an effective way to let people share their reactions without prying into their journals. Free expression by the group members is facilitated, and the counselor has contact with their impressions as recorded in the journals.

I believe that communication between group meetings should be channeled by the counselor into the group session. This belief comes from the axiom that counselors should not see group members in individual counseling while a group is in progress.

For Use with Adolescents

As I explained earlier, begin the initial session with the purpose of the group, procedural guidelines, and a brief description of the values clarification process, its stages and substages. Then spend some time getting to know each other. Name tags might be helpful during the first session. I usually tell the group that they should know the first name of every person in the group by the end of the session.

Adolescents will often be more hesitant to reveal their thoughts and feelings than children, especially during the initial session. It will take more effort on the part of the counselor to get past the initial awkwardness among adolescents than with children. As with children, use simple, low threat exercises first and then move to the more complex, high threat exercises later. In this way, trust among the members can develop gradually. An example of moving from lower threat to higher threat is using the parts of "Value Survey."

"Value Survey" is an exercise that creates much thought and discussion among adolescents. This exercise is the "Value Survey" devised by Milton Rokeach. It consists of a list of eighteen terminal values on the top of the page and a list of eighteen instrumental values on the bottom of the page. Adolescents regard this exercise as a tough one, which means that they really have to think during the exercise. This is in contrast to an exercise such as "Values Voting," which most adolescents believe is easy and perhaps childish. The counselor may have to remind the group that even though an exercise is easy, it can be very useful. In "Value Survey," each group member must rank eighteen values in the order in which each value is important to him. The values include equality, freedom, happiness, an exciting life, family security, and so on. Then each member tells his top three or four values and what reasons led him to rank them so highly. The counselor and the group may question each member. The counselor can compare and contrast each person's values with those of other group members. Completion of the second half of the exercise is a bit more threatening.

In the second half of the "Value Survey," members individually rank eighteen characteristics listed on a page before them. These characteristics are to be ranked in the order in which the member wants each of them to apply to him. The characteristics include terms such as ambitious, cheerful, honest, intellectual, and so on. The counselor can then have each member read his three top-ranked characteristics aloud. Comparison and contrast discussion may then take place among the group.

VALUE SURVEY

Most Important Values to Me

_____ A Comfortable Life   _____ Inner Harmony
_____ A Sense of Accomplishment   _____ Mature Love
_____ A World of Beauty   _____ National Security
_____ A World of Peace   _____ Pleasure
_____ An Exciting Life   _____ Salvation
_____ Equality   _____ Self-Respect
_____ Family Security   _____ Social Recognition
_____ Freedom   _____ True Friendship
_____ Happiness   _____ Wisdom

Important Means by Which to Achieve Values

_____ Ambitious   _____ Imaginative
_____ Broadminded   _____ Independent.
_____ Capable   _____ Intellectual
_____ Cheerful   _____ Logical
_____ Clean   _____ Loving
_____ Courageous   _____ Obedient
_____ Forgiving   _____ Polite
_____ Helpful   _____ Responsible
_____ Honest   _____ Self-Controlled

An additional technique may then be used which is to ask each member if he believes that he now possesses these top-ranked characteristics. Then the counselor can tell each member that he may request feedback from the group as to their opinions of how much each member possesses his top-ranked characteristics. Each member could then be polled by the counselor as to whether he wanted feedback from the group. A more directive counselor would not give members the option of requesting feedback but move directly into feedback for each group member.

Each of the three parts of the "Value Survey" exercise (ranking terminal values, ranking means of obtaining terminal values, and feedback) is important when used alone or in sequence. The threat level or level of anxiety does increase with each of the three phases of the exercise and has contributed to the success of its use with adolescents. Young people see that each part is related to each other and that the concept of values is very important in their lives.

I usually introduce an exercise by saying that we are going to do an exercise that will help us identify our likes and dislikes or value indicators. We then move into the exercise very quickly before everyone wants to become an observer. Adolescents have the verbal skills to do exercises without the help of pencil and paper, but such aids do help any exercise. The exercises used in the *prizing* stage with adolescents are the same as those used with children. The difference is that adolescents will discuss the issues raised by the exercises more deeply than will children.

A technique that I have found to be effective with adolescents is "Values Continuum." The counselor selects the opposite ends of the room which the group uses as opposite ends of a continuum. The counselor also designates a midpoint on the continuum and stands there. Group members are to position themselves along the continuum according to the degree to which they identify or agree with the questions read by the counselor. Questions would include "What do you do with your money?", with one end of the continuum designated as "spend it all" and the other end as "save it all." Members walk to that point on the imaginary line that represents their answer to the question. In *Values Clarification* the ends of the continuum are designated by clever names such as "Hoarding Hannah" and "Handout Helen." I do not use these names, since group members often laugh at the names and continue laughing throughout the exercise, thereby minimizing the impact of the exercise. The exercise is fun, but I do not think the clever names add anything to the exercise and can sometimes reduce its effectiveness. This exercise shows visibly that people have different values, and it involves physical action which adolescents like. Much discussion of similarities and differences of values is stimulated.

Another effective technique with adolescents, and as equally nonthreatening as "Values Continuum," is the "Suitcase Strategy." In this exercise the counselor tells the group to imagine that they are going to work together for a year in a foreign country. During this year they will be isolated from any verbal or written communication with the outside world. They can take only one suitcase, so they must list the items they would take with them. Once they make their list, they share the items with the rest of the group members. Members really think seriously about the important items in their lives and often take mementoes of past activities such as a party or special event in their lives.

One other exercise that has a different effect and is a powerful stimulus is "Life Boat." Each group member is given a list of passengers on a cruise ship from America to England. The list has information such as age, sex, political and moral background, occupation, etc. on all passengers. The counselor tells the group that the ship sinks and the life boat will hold all the passengers except one. Each group member is to decide individually which person will not be allowed to enter the life boat. When each person has chosen one of the passengers, he or she tells the group which one has been chosen and the reasons for doing so.

PASSENGER LIST OF AMERICA TO ENGLAND VOYAGE

Salesman — 56; married, 5 childen ages 9 to 17; going to Israel to help with certain industrial development; a leader in his community.

Black Panther Leader — 25; single; enroute to England to organize Black Panther contingents among oppressed British blacks and to train people for leadership positions in the revolution.

Doctor — 63; married; 3 children over 21; gave up lucrative practice because he believes he has discovered a possible cure for leukemia.

Women's Liberation Leader — 34; single; going to France to address international meeting of advocates for the advancement of equality for women.

Stewardess — 22; single.

Roustabout — 47; single; gambler; former ship captain; excellent knowledge about the sea.

Musician — 41; black; blind; enroute to Europe for concert tour.

Nun — 28; single, teacher who is a specialist in teaching mentally retarded children.

Farmer — 43; married; on his way to Africa to work with A.I.D.; excellent hunter and fisherman; former Marine with knowledge of survival training; had suffered heart attack two years ago.

Student — 20; single; going to Sweden to evade draft.

Peace Corps Member — 24; married; returning to her post and husband after visiting a sick parent; married 3 months.

Nurse (Call Girl) — 29; single, has entered new profession during the last two years as it seems to be more profitable; she is four months pregnant.

CIA Agent — 36; married; 2 children aged 1 and 2; about to leave government work; has vital information memorized concerning a government overthrow in Algeria.

Fugitive — 34; single; former Ivy League college professor; escaped from prison where he was serving sentence for sale, transporting, possession, and use of dangerous drugs; seeks asylum in foreign country where he will renounce U.S. citizenship.

Minister — 43; married, no children; a civil rights leader who is going to Europe to receive an award.

Teacher — 26; single; leave of absence to study in Paris; great writing potential.

Interior Decorator — 40; homosexual.

Child — 11; going to boarding school in France; very wealthy family; crippled from birth.

Banker — 43; 6 children, ages 10 to 21; leading John Birch member who is going to France to discuss with various politicians leaving the United Nations.

Widow — 73; enroute to Italy to fulfill promise to dying husband that she would visit their old home once more. Trip cost her their life's savings.

There are several techniques similar to this one, such as "Fallout Shelter" and perhaps "Cave-in Simulation." I really dislike the notion of telling the group to decide a life or death situation as in "Life Boat," "Fallout Shelter," or "Cave-in," and I tell the group my feelings. However, both "Life Boat" and "Fallout Shelter" have been so effective that I tolerate my feelings of discomfort. With "Cave-in Simulation" there is a slightly different problem which keeps me from using this exercise.

In "Cave-in," the counselor tells the group they are trapped in a cave, but there is a tunnel to safety. The members must go through the tunnel single file, and those near the front will reach the outside first. Each member must give reasons why he should be placed at the front of the line and thus have the greatest chance for survival. Philosophically, I do not believe any person needs to or should justify his existence to anyone else other than perhaps himself. This exercise asks for such a justification, which I find unnecessary and personally objectionable.

One final strategy that can be very worthwhile is "Unfinished Sentences," with stems selected specifically for an adolescent population. One form of "Unfinished Sentences" is shown here.

Unfinished Sentences for Adolescents

1. If I were five years older, I . . .
2. I am best when . . .
3. In a group I . . .
4. I often wish that I . . .
5. My parents are usually . . .
6. I don't like people who . . .
7. What I want most in life is to be . . .
8. My brother (sister) and I are . . .
9. Girls are often . . .
10. With my friends I usually . . .
11. I am most happy when I . . .
12. Boys can be very . . .
13. My friends think that I . . .
14. With my teachers I try to be . . .
15. If I could be different I would . . .

I often use this exercise as a homework assignment to be done between sessions at home. The group would share their answers in pairs to begin with and then with the whole group. I have them share in pairs initially, since some of the sentences deal with sensitive topics such as opposite-sex friendships, sibling relationships, and so on. After sharing with one person in a pair, members are often more ready to share with the entire group.

Guidelines for Discussion

As I stated before, the key to successful use of any exercise is the discussion following the exercise. Avoid asking questions where the socially desirable answer is very obvious. Adolescents may often want the socially desirable or appropriate value, but

help them see that other values exist. Challenge the values or
value indicators listed by the group so they can see that their
values or value indicators are only part of the many that exist
and are acceptable.

I suggest that you compare and contrast the values prized by
different members of the group. Adolescents are often relieved
that their peers have values or value indicators (likes and dislikes) similar to theirs. In addition, they can learn that where
they differ from their peers is an acceptable and even valuable
aspect of their unique identity.

Furthermore, the group should focus on areas such as
leisure-time interests, school, parents, part-time work, dating,
relationships with adults, which are so important to adolescents. I know one counselor who always uses the question
"How would your parents feel about your values?" as a way of
sparking interest in a group of adolescents.

Additional Guidelines

More specifically, make sure everyone in the group has a
chance to speak. You might have to restrain an overly enthusiastic person so that a more reluctant member can speak to the
group. Sometimes those reluctant adolescents look as if they are
going to respond but do not. The facial cues and body posture
that indicate that a person wishes to speak should be recognized
by the counselor. I would call on such a person and ask if he
wished to say something. Even if a silent member is devoid of
facial cues I would call on him in order to get him more involved with the group. I believe that silent members of any
group can profit from the group, but they do not help others in
the group by their silence. If a person were silent for the first
two or three sessions, I would speak to him after the group
meeting and ask if he could contribute more. If he still did not
communicate I would remove him from the group. He can be
put into another values group or a counseling group or be seen
in individual counseling.

Some members will make unusual responses to gain attention; others make such responses because they see the world

differently than most adolescents. If group members do make unusual responses, be as accepting and as tolerant as you can be. If you accept strange responses, you will quickly become a powerful person in their lives. Be accepting, plus reward them by verbal praise for making statements that may sound unusual to us as adults but that may be acceptable to adolescents.

If unusual or atypical comments appear to detract the group from its tasks, you may wish to focus the group's attention to this person's behavior as many experienced counselors would do. This approach allows the group to help a specific member examine his behavior as seen by other persons in the group. For most counselors, especially inexperienced ones, I suggest that you speak to the member who makes distracting comments outside the group in order to reduce the number of his distracting comments. In this way group sessions are used for purposes of value clarification per se, not specific behavior changes deemed necessary by the counselor.

Another suggestion is to learn to live with inconsistency. During adolescence, boys and girls have dramatic and rapid changes in their stated beliefs. They may contradict themselves from session to session of a values group, and we must not be critical of them for their behavior. I believe that adolescents are not sure about what they believe, and so they change their statements in order to test their beliefs. They "try on" beliefs and test them by viewing the reactions of others toward them. This "trying on" process is reasonable and valuable for them even though it may be quite confusing for counselors and other adults. If we are aware of this inconsistency among adolescents, then we may be able to respond more openly to them and help them toward consistency.

Somewhat similar to the statement on inconsistency is the suggestion that you accept ambivalence among adolescents. Ambivalence refers to the condition where group members have both positive and negative feelings about an activity, a person, or a value at the same time. This condition is certainly acceptable and quite logical, since some people like to eat spaghetti because of the taste but do not like the calories it contains. Realization by adolescents that their ambivalence is normal and even indicative of emotional maturity and sophistication can be very reassuring to them. Such a realization should be made clear by the counselor.

Summary

In this chapter I have described the practical aspects of introducing values clarification techniques to children and adolescents and then some guidelines for conducting the discussion following the use of a technique. All of the techniques designed for the *prizing* stage of values clarification need to be examined before you begin a group. Select those techniques with which you feel most comfortable.

Most beginning counselors will find the suggestions in this chapter too general. Experienced counselors may find them too specific or simplistic. The suggestions concerning introducing a technique and discussion following a technique are designed to give a structured plan that may be followed closely by beginning counselors or modified radically by experienced counselors.

In addition, the suggestions made in this chapter emphasize the discussion that follows an exercise rather than the exercise itself. The prizing of a value in a values clarification technique is not important unless the prizing statement is examined by and compared to those of other members of the group. Once accurate identification has been made in the *prizing* stage, refinement can be made by means of the techniques associated with the *choosing* stage.

References

Simon, S., Howe, L., & Kirschenbaum, H.: *Values Clarification: A Handbook of Practical Strategies for Teachers and Students.* New York, Hart, 1972.

CHAPTER IV

USING THE CHOOSING STAGE

Introduction

In the *choosing* stage of the values clarification process, three substages are found. These substages are *choosing from alternatives, choosing after consideration of consequences,* and *choosing freely.* These substages can be viewed as three decision-making skills that are necessary for making rational and potentially satisfying decisions. These skills are taught to the children or adolescents by the counselor, practiced in the group, and then applied outside the group. The teaching process is cognitive, and so the *choosing* stage is usually more cognitive than the *prizing* stage.

In another way, the *choosing* stage consists of having young people make finer distinctions among the values that they identified during the *prizing* stage. Not only do they make distinctions but also they categorize their values in terms of most important to least important. During this stage, persons individually examine their values rather than compare them with those of others as they did during the *prizing* stage — an intracomparison rather than an intercomparison so to speak.

Perhaps the most important conceptual part of this stage is that there is an examination of the behaviors that stem from the stated values. For example, honest people return the toys or books they borrow. This is not just a matter of definition of values terms but an educative experience for young people which gives reality to their values.

Since the focus is on the learning of decision-making skills in this stage, I believe that the counselor role takes on some teacher characteristics. In other words, the counselor teaches the skills, critiques the learning, and helps young people critique each other. Most counselors are directive or task oriented with this stage which will not be inhibiting to the participants.

53

Many counselors and teachers have taken some of the decision-making skills of the *choosing* stage and developed them apart from the values clarification process. This is a reasonable plan except that the relationship between decisions and values is important and should be shown to students through all three substages and shown in sequence. Using just the *choosing* stage is valuable but not as valuable as using this stage in connection with the *prizing* and *acting* stages.

In this chapter I will give guidelines on introducing exercises used during the *choosing* stage, what exercises might be used, how to sequence them, and discussion questions to use after the exercises.

Substages of Choosing

Choosing from Alternatives

The substage called *choosing from alternatives* has two essential aspects. First, there are alternatives from which we can choose. Even though we may not like the alternatives, there are alternatives! For example, we have often heard a child or adolescent say, "But I had to stay home from school! I couldn't do anything else!" Actually, there may have been a variety of choices, but the young person may have been unaware of them or had not taken time to think of them. By learning to seek alternatives from other people or to take time to think of other alternatives alone, a person may improve the chances of making a satisfying decision.

Secondly, if we learn to generate alternatives rather than accept the obvious choice, then we may be able to find choices that are more satisfying to us. Many times a person has said that he took the obvious course of action rather than examine a variety of options. An "obvious course of action" may mean "easiest" or "imposed by others" depending on a person's particular life situation. People can choose the path of least resistance or choose an option desired by their friends, but if they learn to think in terms of alternatives, they may be more likely to make choices that are consistent with their values. I do not believe that we always make choices that are consistent with our values. Indeed, we let environmental contingencies influence us to make an "obvious," "easy," or "imposed" choice. The techniques associated with the *choosing from alternatives* substage can teach people to find options that are consistent with their values.

Choosing with Knowledge of Consequences

The *choosing with knowledge of consequences* substage is closely related to the *choosing from alternatives* substage that precedes it. After learning to seek alternatives, a person must then learn to evaluate each alternative in order to make an eventual selection among them. By listing the positive or negative outcomes of each alternative, a person can quickly arrive at the one that is most satisfying.

There are several complex parts of this substage. One part is that children and adolescents must think in terms of hypothetical outcomes; that is, what might happen. Examining the consequences of alternatives is really guessing what consequences might occur. This is difficult for children, but group members can help by telling how they see the possible consequences.

Another complex aspect is the difference between the short-term and long-term consequences. Often, children and adolescents choose an alternative based solely on the immediate or short-term consequences. A youngster may fight in the schoolyard to get revenge, to release aggressive urges, and to save face among the onlookers (short-term consequences) without considering the long-term consequences such as being punished if caught, guilt over hurting someone, or being avoided by other children who fear him. Some theorists of developmental psychology use a child's ability to examine long-term consequences of behavior as an index of maturity. The skill of looking at long-term consequences can be learned by children and adolescents through techniques and discussion among each other.

One final complexity is that some children and adolescents

behave in ways that have a high probability of success regardless of the nature of the act which might be harmful to others and inconsistent with their values. I know of many youth in inner-city areas who have been so lacking of success experiences with the resulting lack of confidence that they would engage in stealing or fighting, where they would be likely to succeed, rather than participate in social relations or school activities. This decision is not indicative of psychological character disorders or traumas but a deep need to feel worthwhile. The logical move to accomplish success, albeit through antisocial activities, can impede a person's examination of values and consequences, since his only criteria for behavior is the probability of success.

I believe that sometimes we act consistently with our values even though we believe that our acts have a low probability for success. Counselors work with people who may have little probability of change. We vote for candidates whom we favor even though the polls say they cannot win the election! When we act only in ways that are likely to be successful, then our value of success or competence is so dominant that we may tend to be rather unidimensional in our lives. A broader range of activities and expression of values may lead to a more satisfying life-style. The future research by sociologists and social psychologists into adult life-styles may be of help in our understanding of this success phenomenon.

Choosing Freely

The *choosing freely* substage is perhaps less complex than the first two substages, but it is a difficult one for children and adolescents to grasp. I believe that the originators of the values clarification process would like to have young people make free choices but are aware that most choices young people make are not truly free. In our Western society, young people are emotionally and financially dependent on others, especially parents, until they are between eighteen and twenty-one years of age. Therefore, to expect this substage to produce young people who make completely free decisions would be unrealistic. The expectation should be, I believe, to help young people to be aware of the influences upon them and to be free of those pressures upon which they can act. They may be able to realize the influences of their friends and make choices that are less dependent upon those influences. They may not, realistically, be able to deny the wishes or influences of their parents.

The values clarification techniques that I believe are most appropriate to the *choosing* stage are listed here by name and number assigned to them in *Values Clarification*. Some of these strategies are also appropriate for the *prizing* stage, described in Chapter III, and the *acting* stage, described in Chapter V, and are included in those chapters. These techniques are also listed in the Appendix by number, name, and page as they appear in *Values Clarification* (Simon et al., 1972), where they are described in detail.

The techniques are "Value Survey" (7), "Values Focus Game" (18), "Partner Risk" or "Sharing Trios" (20), "Privacy Circles" (21), "Risk Ratio" or "Force-field Analysis" (22), "Alternatives Search" (23), "Alternative Action Search" (24), "Brainstorming" (25), "Consequences Search" (26), "Pattern Search" (29), "Three Characters" (30), "Chairs or Dialogue with Self" (31), "Percentage Questions" (32), "The Pie of Life" (33), "Pages for an Autobiography" (36), "Unfinished Sentences" (37), "Strength of Values" (39), "Sensitivity Modules" (45), "Personal Coat of Arms" (47), "Rogerian Listening" (51), "The Free Choice Game" (52), "Obituary" (56), "Two Ideal Days" (57), "Life Inventory" (58), "How Would Your Life be Different?" (60), "Clothes and Values" (64), "The Miracle Workers" (66), "Ways to Live" (67), "Past Christmas Inventory" (69), "Ready for Summer" (71), "Brand Names" (74), "Baker's Dozen" (75), and "Diaries" (77).

For Use with Children

I believe that the counselor in a values group composed of children must use simple examples of events that all members of the group have examined. Most children have been in a situation at home or in school where they had a choice of tattling on a friend or remaining silent to keep the friendship intact. Many children have taken candy or money from their parents or siblings without permission rather than directly ask for some. These situations may be overused examples of moral dilemmas, but they are real and illustrative to children. The purpose of selecting situations such as the two mentioned above or others described in strategies such as "Alternative Action Search" is not to find the right alternative but to help children learn that there are alternatives available to them. For this reason I use "Alternative Action Search" initially to help children become aware of the many choices available to people.

In "Alternative Action Search" the counselor reads a one-paragraph story that has no ending. A typical story would describe a child in a supermarket who observes a mother hitting a child for knocking down some cans. Group members are asked to decide what they would do if they had observed the incident, tell their decision to the group, and discuss their reasons for their decision. I would put minimal emphasis on their reasons and quickly ask what else could have been done that would hopefully allow them to generate other alternative actions. Then I would ask them about their reaction to the many alternatives we devised. Are they surprised at the large number? Would they have thought of so many alone? Are there people they know who would do each of these actions? Use only two or three unfinished stories so that the children realize that many alternatives are available in every situation.

A strategy that can follow "Alternative Action Search" is "Alternatives Search." In this technique group members devise alternatives or ways of acting in a situation given to them by the counselor. Sample situations or issues would be ways of making friends, how to avoid fighting, helping adults, becoming more confident, or how to have more fun after school. During this exercise, children talk about what is hypothetically possible for a person to do in order to make friends. This helps them learn to be more creative in their thinking. By thinking of what might be possible, they are expanding their realm of options for their own lives. This exercise is similar to "Brainstorming," which I would use with adolescents in place of "Alternatives Search."

One basic rule I use when introducing any exercise to help children generate alternatives is to make the process an exciting discovery. I believe that the strategies can be exciting if the leader is enthusiastic. The idea of discovery seems to motivate the children by arousing their curiosity. In addition, I emphasize that the answers we discover are not right or wrong. This is difficult for many children to accept at first; but when they see that you are accepting all responses they will be more free to express their alternatives.

Spontaneity is a quality I try to elicit among children without having everyone in the group talk at once in a chaotic fashion. I suggest that you review your rule of only one person speaking at a time before any exercise that might be very stimulating to them. The goal of spontaneous discussion where children speak freely yet do not interrupt or all talk at once is difficult to achieve, but it is more likely to be achieved as the group progresses through a series of meetings.

The *choosing with knowledge of consequences* substage should be introduced differently than the *choosing from alternatives* substage. I believe that children should be approached in a serious but friendly tone and be asked to imagine what might happen if they chose one of two different alternatives. Stress the free and open process of imagining. You can use the word *guessing* instead of *imagining.*

Describe the difference between positive and negative consequences, but use terms such as *pleasant* and *unpleasant* (not *good* and *bad*) instead of *positive* and *negative* so they will understand what you mean. Categorizing consequences into pleasant and unpleasant will be hard for some children, since they do not typically think of labeling consequences at all. To these children, consequences just happen and are experienced without deciding whether the consequence has a label on it.

One exercise that is of value in the *choosing with knowledge of consequences* substage is "Consequences Search." There is no exercise that I would use as a substitute for this particular technique or as an addition to it. Other exercises should be developed to accomplish the goal of this substage. With children I suggest that this technique be done in two phases. In the first phase read a one-paragraph unfinished story to the group and have each person individually pick an alternative to consider. The particular alternative is unimportant. Ask the group to suggest an alternative to consider as a group, then select one that has some support from most of the group which should take no more than a minute. With a chalkboard or large piece of construction paper, draw two columns with one entitled "pleasant" and the other "unpleasant." You may wish to use + or − with the older students. Next have the children spontaneously suggest outcomes of the alternative action under discussion and have them categorize each outcome according to pleasant or unpleasant. Record each outcome on the chalkboard or paper.

After three or more outcomes have been recorded under each heading, move into a more structured discussion of what they learned from doing the exercise. The number of outcomes or whether there are more pleasant outcomes than unpleasant outcomes is not as important as the notion that such outcomes exist and can be examined. Compare the consequences of this particular alternative, and tell the group that this process can also be done for several alternatives and is the basis for choosing one alternative over another. Repeat the entire exercise with a new unfinished story and a new alternative. Remember that the purpose of the exercise is to have children become skilled at imagining a variety of long- and short-term consequences.

The second phase of this exercise is to generate possible outcomes (pleasant and unpleasant) for two or more alternatives. With children you would read an unfinished story, have the group pick two alternative actions that the main character in the story might choose, write down the pleasant and unpleasant outcomes for the first alternative, and record the pleasant and unpleasant outcomes for the second alternative. Recording the consequences should not take any longer than five minutes for each alternative. Lastly, the two alternatives are compared, specifically at first and then more generally in order to help the children understand that this process is effective in their everyday lives. More specific questions for discussion are found later in this chapter.

The third substage of the *choosing* stage is *choosing freely.* This substage has several exercises that are appropriate such as, "How Would Your Life be Different," "Unfinished Sentences," "Are You Someone Who," "Clothes and Values," "Ready for Summer," "Patterns Search," "The Life Choice Game," and "Board of Directors" (described in the section on adolescents). The goals of this substage are to have children understand how much and by whom their values and actions are influenced. For children, a specific example must be selected, such as the time when they wanted to play ball and their friends convinced them to throw stones at cars instead. Or when they wanted to play with friends instead of going directly home from school but went directly home anyway. Through such an example, children can discuss how much they are influenced by other people. By using "Unfinished Sentences" or "Are You Someone Who," you might survey the sources of influence in the children's lives.

Unfinished Sentences

Fill in the spaces to make a complete sentence that best describes you.

 1. Sometimes I don't do everything that . . .
 2. My friends sometimes convince me to . . .
 3. My rights at home are limited by . . .
 4. I'd like to change my teacher's mind about . . .
 5. My choice of clothes depends on . . .
 6. How long my hair gets is decided by . . .
 7. My friends can't change my mind to . . .
 8. One book that really impressed me was . . .
 9. I wish I had more freedom in . . .
10. If I had more influence over my friends, I would . . .
11. A hero I have is . . .
12. One thing I've done to be like my older brother/sister is . . .
13. Most of the time my after-school activities are determined by . . .
14. The person I've dreamed about being similar to is . . .
15. A person whose influence I'd like to reduce is . . .
16. I'm usually honest except when . . .
17. Of my mother and father, the person who affects me most is my . . .
18. If I needed help in making a decision I would ask . . .
19. Television has influenced me by . . .
20. If I can't make a free choice I feel . . .

Other sentence stems could be used as a homework assignment between sessions. Since this exercise takes some writing skill, it is probably more effective with older children.

Are You Someone Who

Circle the letter that best fits you. Y = Yes N = No M = Maybe
Are you someone who . . .

Yes　No　Maybe

Y　N　M　　1. always goes along with what your friends want to do?

Y　N　M　　2. is influenced by your parents about what TV programs to watch?

Y　N　M　　3. sometimes lets other people decide what game to play?

Y　N　M　　4. never believes an answer to a question if it disagrees with your own answer?

Y　N　M　　5. usually agrees with a friend rather than argues with him?

Y　N　M　　6. often disobeys your parents when you know you won't get caught?

Y　N　M　　7. listens to a teacher if you really like her or him?

Y　N　M　　8. lies to protect a friend from being punished for cheating in school?

Y　N　M　　9. buys brand-name products regardless of the higher cost?

Y　N　M　　10. wears the style of clothes that your friends wear?

Y　N　M　　11. has your hair the length you want it?

Y　N　M　　12. would make the decision about having braces on your teeth if you need them?

Y　N　M　　13. decides whether or not your grades in school are high enough?

Y　N　M　　14. has determined whether you're going to participate in organized sports or not?

Y　N　M　　15. has decided on when you will do your homework at night?

Y　N　M　　16. has a choice about what you eat for dinner?

Y　N　M　　17. decides when you will go to bed at night?

Yes   No   *Maybe*

Y	N	M	18. would buy a record that your friends don't like?
Y	N	M	19. writes a book report on a book the teacher liked but you didn't?
Y	N	M	20. tries to do things like your older brother or sister?

Both of the exercises shown above stimulate active discussion and promote insight into the sources of influence and amount of influence on the free choices of children's activities.

Guidelines for Discussion

I believe that the discussion during the exercise and the discussion following the exercise should be qualitatively different. During an exercise, the focus should be on what a child might do if he were in a hypothetical situation or what a person in an unfinished story might do. There is an emphasis on the hypothetical interaction so that children will feel free to fantasize and think creatively regarding choices, their consequences, and sources of influence. Without the anxiety of having to tell what he would do in a situation, a child will be able to easily generate alternatives and estimate consequences.

In addition, there is a focus during the *choosing from alternatives* and *choosing with knowledge of consequences* substages on ideal situations. Not only are hypothetical situations posed, but also many of the situations are idealized in that the cruel facts of reality are temporarily held in abeyance. By suggesting that children think about what might be, we can help them approach the idea of generating alternatives and estimating consequences without being restricted by those factors in life such as racial prejudice, socioeconomic status, etc., which can limit the probability of achieving their alternatives. The purpose of the exercises is to examine alternatives and consequences as freely as possible and to look at limits and sources of influences.

In contrast to the discussion during an exercise that is hypothetical and idealized, the discussion following an exercise should shift to personal examples that would come from the children, not the counselor. After children have generated alternatives and examined consequences, they should discuss situations in their own lives where they might generate alternatives and examine consequences. In other words, the discussion should move from the impersonal to the personal to have children see how the skills learned in the counseling session can be applied to their daily lives.

When children have discussed how skills of generating alternatives and assessing consequences can be used outside the group, they can use the skills on their own. If they need the additional emotional support of a counselor, the counselor can see the child or children individually or in a group, but after the conclusion of the values group. It is better for the counselor and the children to avoid the confusion of meeting individually or in a counseling group at the same time as a values group.

Additional Guidelines

In the discussions following an exercise, I suggest that you urge everyone to participate so you are able to see if they understand the skills they have been practicing. Try to accept all choices they present, even though you do not believe they would actually make such a choice.

Furthermore, if children do not suggest alternatives or consequences or sources of influence that you believe are obvious, make the suggestion yourself. Do not explore their reasons for not mentioning an obvious possibility, but move ahead with the discussion as if the children themselves had mentioned it. In this way you can provide data when necessary as a resource person, rather than a teacher, which places more responsibility on the children to respond in the group.

You might also suggest alternatives such as assertive behavior, or consequences such as physical harm, or sources of influence such as television stars which may be unusual or atypical for some children. The purpose of your atypical suggestions is to expand their conceptions of what alternatives are available even if they do not choose them, what consequences are possible even if not probable, or what sources of influences are present even if not applicable to everyone. This expansion of their view of the world can be helpful to children later in life when they face situations where atypical alternatives can be useful, where unusual consequences may be probable, and where minor sources of influences become major.

For Use with Adolescents

In a similar way to that of working with children, you should help adolescents learn skills involved in the *choosing* stage, not specific values or behaviors per se. Of course, you will choose exercises that are specific and relevant to the adolescents in your group. Working with adolescents is easier for many counselors, since adolescents have more life experiences than children and can use these experiences in understanding the exercises you choose for the group.

In the *choosing from alternatives* substage, adolescents are generally aware of more alternatives than children and can move through this stage quickly. Use of the "Brainstorming" strategy would be appropriate to help the group members to increase their range of alternatives. The counselor would pose a hypothetical situation such as, "Let's say a person was concerned about getting along better with his or her teachers at school; what things could he or she do to improve their relationship?" The emphasis is on creativity, not reality, at this point. Once you have generated a list that you or a group member records, you can stress that the group can often generate more alternatives than can one member acting alone. This indicates the strength of the group and encourages cooperation and cohesiveness. Incidentally, recording the alternatives seems to suggest a seriousness or purpose that sometimes does not occur when no recording is made.

Since adolescents have the capacity for higher levels of abstraction than children, I would use exercises such as "Value Survey," "Strength of Values," or "Ways to Live," which all focus the group members on deciding among alternative values, behavioral patterns, or life-styles.

An exercise that I have found to be successful with adolescents who are capable of higher levels of abstractions is "Value

Survey," which was described in Chapter III. "Value Survey" would be used to help adolescents compare their individual ranking of the eighteen terminal values and the eighteen instrumental values in the exercise. If this exercise were used in the *prizing* stage, the emphasis would be on identifying and discussing the top three or four values in each of the terminal and instrumental categories to help people understand that they do have some preferred values.

In using "Value Survey," have each person in the group take a "Value Survey" sheet, as shown in Chapter III, and rank the five most important values among the eighteen terminal values at the top of the page from one to five. Then have each person rank the least important values from fourteen to eighteen. I suggest that you do not take the time to discuss all eighteen values, although many people will want to rank all eighteen and will do so. After the ranking is done, have the group members share their top rankings with each other, their reasons for choosing these values, and how they act on these values in their daily experiences. The next step would be to discuss the lowest ranked values and why they are not very important. Remember to emphasize that persons should choose values that are important or unimportant according to their individual beliefs, not what others want them to choose. You may then repeat these procedures with the eighteen instrumental values on the bottom half of the "Value Survey" sheet.

I have also used "Miracle Workers" with effectiveness. In this exercise each adolescent is given a sheet of fifteen miracle workers and asked to *circle* the number of the three miracle workers whose magical skills he would most like to possess. After this is done, have the group members, without discussion, *square* the number of the three miracle workers whose services he would least like to use. Next, discuss their circles and their thoughts about their choices. Finally, move into a discussion of their squares. Some group members will also qualify their answers according to short- or long-term goals for themselves, which can be considered in your general discussion with the group.

THE MIRACLE WORKERS

A group of fifteen experts, considered miracle workers by those who have used their services, have agreed to provide these services to you. Their extraordinary skills are guaranteed to be 100 percent effective. It is up to you to decide which of these people can best provide you with what you want. The experts are as follows:

1. Dr. Dorian Grey — A noted plastic surgeon, he can make you look exactly as you want to look by means of a new, painless technique. Your ideal physical appearance can be reality. You can even be shorter or taller.

2. Baron VonBarrons — A college placement and job placement expert. The college or job of your choice, in the location of your choice, will be yours!

3. Jedediah Methuselah — Guarantees you long life (to be the age of 200) with your aging process slowed down. For example, at the age of sixty you will look and feel like twenty.

4. Dr. Johnson — Expert in the area of sexual relations, they guarantee that you will be the perfect male or female, will enjoy sex, and will bring pleasure to others.

5. Dr. Yin Yang — A medical expert. He will provide you with perfect health and protection from physical injury throughout your life.

6. Dr. Knot Ginott — An expert in dealing with parents, he guarantees that you will never have any problems with your parents again. They will accept your values and your behavior. You will be free from control and hassles.

7. Stu Denpower — An expert on authority, he will make sure that you are never again bothered by authorities. His services will make you immune from all control that you consider unfair by the school, the police, and the government.

8. "Pop" Larity — He guarantees that you will have the friends you want now and in the future. You will find it easy to approach those you like and they will find you easily approachable.

9. Dr. Charlie Smart — He will develop your common sense and your intelligence to a level highest in the class.

10. Rocky Fellah — Wealth will be yours. You will earn over a million dollars within weeks.

11. Dwight D. DeGawl — This world famed expert on leadership will train you. You will be listened to, looked up to, and respected by those around you.

12. Dr. Otto Carnegy — You will be well-liked by all. You will never be lonely. A life filled with love will be yours.

13. Dr. Claire Voyant — All of your questions about the future will be answered, continually, through the training of this miracle worker.

14. Dr. Hannah Self — Guarantees that you will have self-confidence. True self-assurance will be yours.

15. Prof. Val U Clear — With his help, you will always know what you want, and you will be completely clear on all confusing issues of these days.

With some adolescents who do not admit that they already operate in rigid ways, it may be useful to precede the "Miracle Workers" exercise or others mentioned with "Patterns Search." In this exercise, group members categorize some behaviors you select, such as gossiping, making friends with the opposite sex, or going along with the crowd, according to whether they act on these behaviors out of compulsion, habit, or free choice. During the discussion, many students realize that they are not compelled into behavior but are acting out of habit or free choice and so can change their actions according to what they really value.

"Patterns Search" would be used in the same way that it would be used for children (described earlier in this chapter), except the patterns you choose for them to examine would be more age-appropriate. With children you might have them see if they have a pattern (done out of compulsion, habit, or free choice) about doing homework, choosing friends, or making friends. With adolescents you might have them check their patterns regarding dating, gossiping, or paying debts.

Once the group has examined some patterns and realized that many alternatives are possible and do exist, they can learn to evaluate the consequences of the alternatives. I suggest that when you use exercises such as "How Would Your Life Be Different," "Ways to Live," "Consequences Search," or "Unfinished Sentences," you should look at possible short-term or immediate consequences first. For many adolescents, immediate consequences occur within a minute or two after they commit an act. They rarely consider consequences that might occur a day or a week later, so you could initially work with the immediate consequences. Furthermore, always use the word *possible* consequences or results. This helps adolescents learn that no consequences are 100 percent inevitable but that some are probable, others possible, and still others improbable. They often find this notion of probability a difficult one to grasp, but when they do grasp it they will have made a significant step toward responsible and independent behavior.

Once you have examined the notion of probability, you may also examine the assumption that all behavior yields some results that are positive or rewarding and some that are negative or unrewarding. I try to avoid labeling the terms *good* or *bad* because of the bias they contain. With an exercise such as "Consequences Search," it is easy to have each group member draw two columns and list the positive results of joining the army, getting married, or finding a part-time job in one column and the negative results in the other column. Group members can compare lists and discuss probabilities and reasons for the results they listed.

Finally, I suggest that you make a distinction between short-term and long-term consequences of various alternative behaviors. You may have to be the major source of input regarding long-term (one day to one week) results if group members have difficulty thinking of long-term results. This perspective can be developed by practice in the group and perhaps by brainstorming about what long-term consequences might result from certain actions. You might also have group members draw two columns on a piece of paper, choose actions such as dropping out of school, fighting with a parent, or seeking help with mathematics, and then list a dozen consequences for them. Their task would be to put each consequence you list in the short-term or long-term column. After you have read all the consequences, the group can compare their lists and the reasons for making their discriminations between short-term and long-term.

The entire *choosing with knowledge of consequences* substage blends quite easily with the *choosing freely* substage, since many adolescents will say that they "can't" choose to do certain things because of what others will say and do to them. The purpose of the *choosing freely* substage is to help adolescents examine the sources of influence on what they do and the amount of influence these sources exert. The assumption is that if adolescents are aware of these influences, more free choices will be made. Of course, there will always be strong influences on all choices we make, but if we are aware of them we may be able to make choices that are more closely in line with our values.

Doctor Leland Howe showed me the "Board of Directors" exercise, which is excellent for the *choosing freely* substage. The worksheet for this exercise is shown in Figure 4.

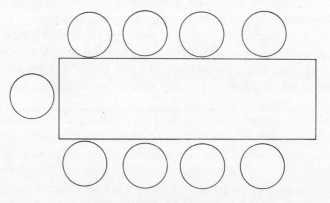

Figure 4. Board of Directors.

You will need to point out the analogy between the way a board of directors of an organization is consulted in making important policy decisions and the "board of directors" (parents, teachers, friends) that each of us consults when we make our own important life decisions. Each group member takes a worksheet on which is drawn a board of directors' table and chairs. Each person's own name is placed at the head of the table as the "chairman of the board." Then each person writes the names of the persons they consult in making important decisions in the chairs around the table. These may be people they consult in person or people whose psychological presence influences them. As many chairs may be filled as the person wishes, and more chairs may be added.

When the adolescents are finished they are to code the names with the following codings:

1. Place three checks (✓ ✓ ✓) beside any person who is almost always consulted, two checks (✓ ✓) beside any person who is frequently consulted, one check (✓) beside any person who is sometimes consulted.

2. Place a *PSY* beside any person whose influence is primarily psychological, for example, an author of a book who has had an impact upon your life and the way you live it. Place a *PHY* beside any person whose physical presence is consulted.

3. Place a *K* beside any person you would like to keep and an *E* beside anyone you would like to eliminate. Percentages may be allocated, e.g. "I'd like to keep 50 percent and eliminate 50 percent of my father's influence."

The purpose of the codings is to get group members to analyze their sources of influence and their process of making decisions. After they have done the codings, you can conduct a comparison among the worksheets of group members, which can lead to a discussion of changing one's sources of influence. Once a young person has analyzed the sources and amounts of influence, he can decide whether or not he is satisfied with that influence. If an adolescent is not satisfied, then you and other group members can help him to discover new sources and ways of reducing old sources. This helping process moves group members into the *acting* stage of the values clarification process very smoothly.

Guidelines for Discussion

In the discussion following any exercise in the *choosing* stage, I try to get group members to think of the alternatives, consequences, and influences of all adolescents, not just themselves. Too often, adolescents have a rigid egocentric position in which they believe that everyone else is like them. Comparing their answers in the exercises to those of the rest of the group helps an adolescent to see the differences between himself and others.

Keep in mind that a positive consequence for one group member may be a negative consequence for another member. An example would be that of social recognition. Some adoles-

cents value actions that result in attention from others, while
other adolescents avoid acts that would direct the spotlight on
them. By showing such differences, you can help adolescents to
see that their value system is an individual one that, when
compared to others' systems, is neither good nor bad, just different. Due to the great conformity of dress, language, and
customs among the adolescent subculture, an understanding
that differences are not horrible but inevitable and worthy of
acceptance is quite mature.

Try to keep the group from being discouraged by the person
who says, "This alternative is no good for you because it didn't
work for me!" The group should be encouraged to evaluate an
alternative based on themselves, not others. Also, the adolescent
who makes such an overgeneralization should be helped to say,
"This alternative is no good *for me* because it didn't work for
me." This statement does not overgeneralize and so is less likely
to inhibit other group members.

In the area of *choosing freely*, I usually move the discussion
toward how the group members can reduce some of the influences on their lives and increase other influences. Avoiding
certain people, reading, making new friends, or joining clubs
can lead to new influences.

Additional Guidelines

I stress the notion of responsible independence among adolescents based on the concept that we do things because of what
we value, not what others value. For example, I urge group
members to make "I" statements rather than "he/she made me
do it" statements. I de-emphasize rebellion for the sake of pun-
ishing parents or teachers and help students to look for alternatives that will have a high probability of short-term and long-
term consequences.

Furthermore, I often have adolescents compare their immediate past with their present in order to help them see if they
are learning from their past experiences. Unfortunately, it
seems that many adolescents are fearful of trying new alternatives even though the old alternatives are usually unsuccessful.

If they learn the strategies of generating new alternatives, examining long-term as well as short-term consequences, and analyzing the sources of influence upon them, they may be more capable of choosing actions that are more satisfying to them.

References

Simon, S., Howe, L., & Kirschenbaum, H.: *Values Clarification: A Handbook of Practical Strategies for Teachers and Students.* New York, Hart, 1972.

CHAPTER V

USING THE ACTING STAGE

VALUES are tied to specific behaviors in the *acting* stage of the values clarification process. The two substages of this stage are *acting* and *acting with consistency*. As I explained in Chapter I, the *acting* substage is designed to help children and adolescents realize that their actions are related to their values. The *acting with consistency* substage is designed to help young people act in a pattern rather than in a random fashion.

There is an assumption in the *acting* substage that people should act on their values rather than espouse values and do nothing about them. I believe that if adults are passive about their espoused values then their espoused values are not at the top of their value system. Children and adolescents are unlike these adults because young people have more constraints upon their actions than adults. Also, many young people do not have the skills in initiating actions that are consistent with their values. Getting started in actions is the biggest part of the *acting* substage. In order to eliminate the blind actions and false starts made with little preparation, exercises are used to help young people act in ways that are most likely to be consistent with their values.

The purpose of the *acting with consistency* substage is to help young people behave in a consistent manner. This purpose is aimed at those children and adolescents who behave in a random, unplanned, and almost completely spontaneous way. I believe there is a high degree of consistency in individual behavior according to how each person views the world and what each person values. I believe that there is less consistency of behavior among children and adolescents than among adults. This lack of consistency can be due to a sense of confusion or to a sense of experimentation among young people. The *acting with consistency* substage is designed for those young people who act out of confusion and doubt.

I spend less time on the *acting* stage than on the *prizing* and *choosing* stages. Action is discussed during the earlier two stages to make the discussions concrete and lively. Furthermore, the primary purpose of values clarification is educative, not remedial. If some young people have major behavior problems other than in getting started or establishing some consistency, they should be referred to a problem-solving group or else to individual counseling. An additional reason for spending more time on the first two stages is to establish a firm basis of knowledge and skills so that the *acting* stage is easily and quickly completed. Furthermore, most children and adolescents are very action-oriented and want to act rather than be planful in their lives.

The values clarification techniques that I believe are most appropriate to the *acting* stage are listed here by name and number assigned to them in *Values Clarification.* Some of these strategies are also appropriate for the *prizing* stage, Chapter III and for the *choosing* stage, Chapter IV, and are included in those chapters. These techniques are also listed in the Appendix by number, name, and page as they appear in *Values Clarification,* where they are described in detail.

The techniques are "Values Grid" (2), "Removing Barriers to Action" (27), "Getting Started" (28), "Unfinished Sentences" (37), "Values in Actions" (42), "Letters to the Editor" (43), "I Urge Telegrams" (44), "Unfinished Business" (46), "Personal Coat of Arms" (47), "Rogerian Listening" (51), "Self Contracts" (59), "Christmas Gift-Giving" (68), "Past Christmas Inventory" (69), "RDA's Resent-Demand-Appreciate" (70), "Ready for Summer" (71), "Diaries" (77), and "Assist Groups or Support Groups" (79).

For Use with Children

Children are generally action-oriented; that is they act quickly on what they value at a particular moment. These children usually have little difficulty in getting started, since their values are expressed in terms of present-oriented behaviors with immediate consequences. They understand, for example, that they value recognition from peers, and when a chance to recite in class appears, they take it. The opportunity was offered by someone else (the teacher) without planning by the child, and the consequence (achieving recognition) was immediate. With some practice, these children can be helped to plan for situations that would give them recognition. However, even the most action-oriented children are blocked sometimes in their expression of values and need help in getting past such blocks.

Exercises such as "Values Grid," "Removing Barriers to Action," "Unfinished Sentences," "Diaries," or "Assist Groups" can help children who need help in getting started. In "Removing Barriers to Action," have the group members each take a piece of paper and fold it in half. On one half have them write a value that is important to them but on which they have not acted. On the other half of the page have them list the reasons (or barriers) why they have not acted on this value. Then let the group share their lists and discuss ways of removing the barriers to action.

In "Getting Started," have the group members each make three columns on a piece of paper. In the first column they should list the areas in which they would like to do things differently such as in school, with friends, with new people, in play activities, or with adults. Then in the second column they assign a future date by which they will have tried to accomplish some activities related to the areas they listed in column one. Then each person writes down in the third column some first steps or actions that relate to an area in column one. Have each person read an area in which he or she would like to do things differently, the date, and the beginning actions or first steps. Other group members can then suggest other actions that can be taken, which the person can record on his sheet in column three. Since so much writing might be difficult for children, many counselors put the three columns on a chalkboard or large piece of construction paper and do the writing for the children.

After using "Removing Barriers to Action" and "Getting

Started," you may then wish to use "Self Contracts," if needed, or "Support Groups." "Self Contracts" is similar to "Getting Started" but is more specific. In "Getting Started," a person may say that he will begin saving money, or try to dress differently, or smile more often. In "Self Contracts," behaviors are written down in a contract fashion and are very specific. A person would write that he will save twenty-five cents per week for the next two months or that he would greet and start a conversation with two new persons at school next week. A person would make the contract, discuss it with you and the group for realism and specificity, sign, and date it. You and the group are needed to help the contract be specific and possible of being accomplished. Some counselors have the contract typed and keep a copy of each person's self-contract. Group members can report to the group periodically regarding their progress.

In order to accomplish the goals of the *acting with consistency* substage, you need to help group members monitor their behavior for a period of time. Activities such as "Diaries" and "Assist or Support Groups" can be most helpful. Any time that children report to the group regarding their progress on a "Self Contract" or "Getting Started" project, a "Support Group" is in effect. A "Support Group" can also be set up by having the group divide into three-person support groups in order to provide a place where a person can turn if help is needed. These small support groups would go into effect at the conclusion of the regularly scheduled values group sessions. An "Assist Group" would be a three-person group established to help a person to accomplish an activity and then report to the total group. This help could be in the form of confronting a bully, helping with homework, or making some attempts at talking to strangers.

"Diaries" is a good technique for group members to record their progress in specific action areas. You might suggest that a person keep a notebook in which he records each time that he avoids a fight, asks an adult for help, or spends money wisely. I usually use the term *log* instead of diary which sounds more acceptable to some children than diary.

Guidelines for Discussion

I believe that there are two main points on which to focus a discussion following an exercise in the *acting* stage. First, it is important to think in terms of the future. In the *prizing* and *choosing* stages the emphasis is on the present, but now the emphasis shifts to the future. If a person has values on which he has not yet acted, what can he do in the immediate future to act in accord with those values?

It is also important to focus on acting as being valuable whether it brings success or failure. If children do not try to remove barriers to action and take some steps at getting started, then perhaps they should examine their stated values to see if they are really so important. Overall, people will not know if their values are really important to them until these values are acted on and evaluated in terms of the consequences that occur. But the consequences cannot be evaluated unless the values are acted upon.

Additional Guidelines

Remember to let the children decide on the actions to be taken even though the actions would not be the ones you would have chosen for yourself. Also, help them to try other behaviors if their first plan brings failure. Such experimentation with new approaches is important, since many children have not been aware that new approaches existed.

One good way to help insure success is by rehearsing behaviors in the group. If a person wants to be more assertive with his friends, then have him practice this behavior with other group members until he becomes proficient. This behavioral rehearsal reduces anxiety and increases skills in a short period of time. Such an exercise takes place in a controlled environment where success is likely to occur. Furthermore, you can critique the action and support the person in his attempts.

For Use with Adolescents

For most adolescents it would be unthinkable to act in ways

that were inconsistent with the norms of their peer group. With other adolescents the most shocking acts are the best to perform. Acting on one's values is difficult for many adolescents, since their most important value is acceptance from their peer group. This acceptance is seen in a desire for conformity, with periodic episodes of attention getting. These behaviors can inhibit actions that are consistent with other values they hold. I believe that adolescent conformity in dress, language, and other behavior is a way of getting acceptance without attracting undue attention, but that their strong desire for recognition and acceptance enables them to tolerate some nonconformity such as acting on other values.

Let me illustrate this point by using an example of an average adolescent who follows the crowd in terms of amount of homework done, use of alcohol or drugs, dating, clothes, and use of spending money. This adolescent may not approve of the behavior of his friends in these areas but conforms because the desire for acceptance is strong. I believe that by using the values clarification process and particularly some exercises in the *acting* stage, this adolescent can be helped to act in ways that are different from the crowd and yet be recognized and valued as one of the group.

For a typical adolescent, barriers to acting on his or her values are either physical (money, time, distance, knowledge, or age) or emotional (fear of rejection or failure). In using techniques such as "Getting Started" or "Removing Barriers to Action" with adolescents, you may wish to mention these categories as a way of directing the group. I would initially focus on physical behaviors then turn to emotional barriers which are often stronger than physical ones.

Similarly, consider the situations in which adolescents are not acting but in which they would like to act. Apathy is a way of not acting, even though an adolescent might like to act. One way of getting apathetic adolescents to act is by using the strategies "Letters to the Editor" or "I Urge Telegrams." In these strategies, adolescents write letters or send telegrams to people to whom they have always wanted to speak. These two techniques are good stimuli for discussions, and the letters and telegrams do not have to be sent.

Once the idea of physical and emotional barriers to acting in certain areas such as home, school, work, or with friends, family, strangers have been discussed, you can have the adolescents list ways of removing the barriers and the specific steps of beginning to act. These ways can be listed individually on paper as in "Getting Started" or "Removing Barriers to Action" or verbally via "Brainstorming," with each member receiving the focus of the entire group.

After a number of suggested actions have been generated, each person should write out a "Self Contract" containing several actions to take within the next week. A person may choose another group member for assistance in accomplishing the actions. The group member should write out the "Self Contract," make a copy for the group leader, and keep a copy. I suggest that actions be generated that will bring results within a week. Often "Self Contracts" fail because the actions are not able to be accomplished within a short period of time. For example, I would change a person's action from "I will get a part-time job" to "I will survey the newspaper want-ads from each evening newspaper this week for possible jobs for which I am qualified" or "I will see my high school counselor about part-time jobs he may know about." At the next group meeting, review each person's success at accomplishing the actions in the "Self Contract." New "Self Contracts" may then be made up for the next week if necessary.

Sometimes "Self Contracts" may take the form of repeated actions such as "I will bring my books to my math class every day this week" or "I will do the dishes every night this week." With some people you may have to reduce the number of consecutive days of action from seven to two or three. This use of "Self Contracts" aids adolescents in becoming more consistent which is the goal of the second substage of the *acting* stage.

Using a log or diary with adolescents can be very effective in helping them take action and maintain some long-term consistency with their values. The diary is especially effective in the interpersonal area if you encourage group members to be free about expressing their feelings in their writings. One suggestion is to have each person keep a specific type of record such as

a "voicing my opinion diary," a "listening to others diary," or
a "making friends diary." In this way the diary will be focused
on the specific actions that each person wants to accomplish.
You should also suggest that the diary will only be kept for a
week or two which frees the adolescents from a long-term
assignment. It is difficult for most adolescents to maintain a
diary for long periods. Of course, if the diary technique is
effective, adolescents will continue to maintain their actions
with some degree of consistency and monitor their behavior in
their minds without the use of a written technique such as a
diary.

One other technique I advocate is "Support Groups." After
the end of the values group sessions, you may have enough
cohesiveness among group members so that they function as
support for each other when they have contact with each other
in school, in the neighborhood, or in other areas. I believe in
periodic follow-up sessions of values groups to encourage
people to use individuals in the group for support. Such
follow-up sessions may occur on a monthly basis or even less
frequently, but their importance for providing continued support is very great.

Guidelines for Discussion

In the discussion following any technique used during the
acting stage, there is an emphasis on doing something outside
the counseling session. During the *prizing* and *choosing* stages
this emphasis was not present. Adolescents may be hesitant to
report on their outside activities, especially concerning failure
to carry out steps designed in the group. You need to give
encouragement at this point and indicate that attempting to
take action (even though the action fails) is worthwhile.

In general, you need to have adolescents try out actions in
order to evaluate if they have learned the principles of the
acting stage. By no means should you (or the adolescents) expect to have the group continue while group members try to
carry out the actions associated with all their values. Such a
group could last for years!

Some adolescents will say that the examples given by you and other group members are not similar to their own life situation. Usually this is a defensive reaction, and you should point out that no one has had the same experience as another person but that we can learn from similar and even opposite experiences. Try to keep this negative reaction from discouraging other group members from listening and trying out actions. This can be accomplished by calling on group members who see the examples as being helpful or similar to their life situations.

You might also find that your adolescents are not defensive but just have trouble understanding similarities. In this case, spend more time citing specific similarities between the examples used in a technique and their personal lives. When examples come from group members themselves, there is a greater probability of their being understood and accepted than if examples come from you.

Another suggestion is to keep from debating the probable success or failure of their actions. As I stated earlier, some adolescents will not attempt action unless they are sure of success. In a relatively short series of values group sessions, you will not be able to have a great deal of impact on such adolescents; therefore, keep a positive tone during the discussions and encourage those adolescents who want to try out some new actions. The other, less confident adolescents can be seen individually by you or another counselor.

A further guideline is to keep the discussion during this stage very brief. I believe that some discussion is necessary to show the group what they can do outside the session, but too much discussion can increase anxiety rather than decrease it. Most of the discussion takes place during the exercise rather than following the exercise. When the exercise is completed, the group members have a plan of action to implement outside the group; therefore, not much discussion is necessary. You may wish to do a role-play in the group to illustrate how actions might take place outside the group. Such an activity can help to build skills and reduce anxiety. This technique should be used if you believe that group members need such help before they leave the group.

Many counselors spend only one or two sessions on this stage, although they will reconvene follow-up sessions later on. If such follow-up sessions show that some people are not carrying out their stated actions and need more attention, referral can be made to individual or group counseling that has a problem-resolution focus. It is important to remember that the focus of all of the values clarification stages is educative, not therapeutic. Children and adolescents learn the skills that can help them in their lives, not just during the crisis periods. The role of the counselor is to help young people to understand and act on what is important to them as individuals. Even though their values may change from childhood through adolescence, the skills of the values clarification process will continue to be valuable.

References

Simon, S., Howe, L., & Kirschenbaum, H.: *Values Clarification: A Handbook of Practical Strategies for Teachers and Students.* New York, Hart, 1972.

VALUES CLARIFICATION TECHNIQUES*

---

*The strategies are listed by number, name, and page number as they appear in S. Simon, L. Howe, H. Kirschenbaum, *Values Clarification: A Handbook of Practical Strategies for Teachers and Students*. (New York, Hart, 1972).

INDEX